13

SHAKESPEARE
AND THE NATURE
OF TIME

SHAKESPEARE AND THE NATURE OF TIME

ᏩᏪᏪᎴ

*Moral and Philosophical Themes
in Some Plays and
Poems of William Shakespeare*

ᏩᏪᏪᎴ

FREDERICK TURNER
M.A. OXON, B.LITT. OXON

OXFORD
At the Clarendon Press
1971

Oxford University Press, Ely House, London W. 1

GLASGOW NEW YORK TORONTO MELBOURNE WELLINGTON
CAPE TOWN SALISBURY IBADAN NAIROBI DAR ES SALAAM LUSAKA ADDIS ABABA
BOMBAY CALCUTTA MADRAS KARACHI LAHORE DACCA
KUALA LUMPUR SINGAPORE HONG KONG TOKYO

PRINTED IN GREAT BRITAIN

Acknowledgements

PROBABLY my greatest debt is to Dame Helen Gardner, for her advice and criticism. They were invaluable in helping me to transform an idea into a book.

I would also like to thank Mr. John Armstrong, now teaching at Eton College, for suggesting many of the insights out of which these chapters began to grow; Mr. J. I. M. Stewart of Christ Church, for his aid and encouragement; and Mr. John Bate, of Napier College, Edinburgh, and Mr. Tom Harding, formerly of the Portsmouth College of Art, for their ideas and comments.

In the later stages of revision Mr. Robert Potter and Mr. William Frost, of the University of California at Santa Barbara, Mr. Edward Casey, of the University of Princeton, and Mr. Reginald Foakes, of the University of Kent, have all been very helpful.

My thanks are due also to the advisers and readers of the Clarendon Press, whose patience and skill have been indispensable, and to Miss Karen Malone, who reduced my foul papers to a typescript.

Finally, I cannot express my gratitude to my father, Mr. Victor Turner, of the Committee on Social Thought at Chicago, and to my wife, who have contributed so much to bringing this book into existence.

Contents

NOTE

ALL line-references unless otherwise stated refer to the play which is the subject of the chapter. E.g. in Chapter 4 all unspecified references refer to *Twelfth Night*; in Chapter 9 all unspecified references refer to *The Winter's Tale*.

The text I have used is Peter Alexander's edition of the *Complete Works* (Tudor Edition, 1964; first published 1951).

1. *Introduction*

A GREAT writer embodies his insights in images which, often enough at first, merely disturb his readers or audience with an obscure sense of their force and truth. But moral awareness shifts and philosophic terminologies alter; and what he captured in parable and symbol may later become accessible to analysis and exposition. Indeed, it is because of such considerations that criticism can improve and progress, where literature itself depends purely on the genius of its creators and cannot evolve in the same way. The critic is limited by the ideas of his time; the poet can transcend, or at least transmute them. But the critic's chief limitation is also his chief asset. As ideas accumulate and evolve, new images of reality appear, and new aspects of old literature may be illuminated.

We have become accustomed in the last century to looking at reality not only as if it were standing still, but also as it moves and changes: we have even begun to consider the motion or change of a thing as part of its nature. The theory of evolution in biology, the ideas of class struggle, political innovation, and economic progress in history, the various psychological theories of conceptual and emotional development in the child and adult, the mathematical concepts of space-time and relativity, are all symptoms and causes of this new awareness of time: especially of time as dynamic, as process and becoming.

That Shakespeare was interested in time as it affects human beings cannot be denied. Most of the Sonnets, as will be shown, deal directly or indirectly with some problem of time. In the *Concordance* there is an extraordinary number of entries under the word 'time' itself. Nor is the word used trivially in most places; often it carries the philosophical and poetic emphasis. Images expressing the nature of time are common in the great soliloquies and philosophical dialogues. The exiles in *As You Like It* 'lose and neglect the creeping hours of time';[1] they 'fleet

---
[1] *As You Like It*, II. vii. 112.

the time carelessly, as they did in the golden world'[2] Viola in
Twelfth Night, discovering that Olivia is in love with her,
declares:

> O Time, thou must untangle this, not I;
> It is too hard a knot for me t' untie![3]

Hamlet, after the Ghost has appeared to him, says bitterly:

> The time is out of joint. O cursed spite,
> That ever I was born to set it right![4]

Macbeth expresses his agony and accidie in the words

> Tomorrow, and tomorrow, and tomorrow, .
> Creeps in this petty pace from day to day
> To the last syllable of recorded time...[5]

and Father Time himself enters at the dramatic pivot of *The
Winter's Tale.*

The present study, then, is concerned with the arsenal of
thoughts, feelings, and attitudes with which Shakespeare attacks
the central problems of man's temporal nature and his relationship with his environment of time. The justification for making
such an addition to the already crowded landscape of Shakespeare
criticism is twofold: that Shakespeare was profoundly interested
in time, and that we are now in a position to understand theoreti-
cally much that was exciting but obscure before.

In writing this study I have not ignored such twentieth-century
notions as appear parallel to the insights contained in the poetry
and drama of Shakespeare. I have not attempted to 'apply'
modern philosophical or scientific concepts of time to the works
of a man who never heard of either; rather, I have tried to suggest
what Shakespeare and the twentieth century have in common in
this respect, and cast light on my object of study by their juxta-
position. And since the language of criticism is perforce the
language of modern rational discourse, such a comparison affords
a method of exposition by which we can translate the language
of poetry, image and symbol, into the language of criticism.

One major modern poem has proved of great use in this
endeavour: *Four Quartets*, by T. S. Eliot. Much of the intellectual

[2] *As You Like It*, I. i. 109.   [3] *Twelfth Night*, II. ii. 38, 39.
[4] *Hamlet*, I. v. 189, 190.   [5] *Macbeth*, V. v. 19 et seq.

structure of the present study has been provided by this poem, which has acted as a catalyst between the poetic world of Shakespeare and the prosaic one of criticism. In his poem Eliot explores the nature of human time profoundly and comprehensively, and in a manner free from the oppressive jargon one sometimes encounters in scientific or philosophical treatments of the theme. At times the comparison between an idea of Shakespeare's and a few lines of *Four Quartets* was irresistible and illuminating.

Time is an immensely complex notion; in this study it displays nine major aspects. Of these the most obvious is historical, objective time, time viewed as from outside it: a space in which events occur. When we look at time in this way we are treating it as if it differs from a spatial dimension only in that it possesses ① direction. Time is the road along which men journey; at certain points on the road events take place. Time in this sense is a means of placing happenings before or after each other, of assigning dates, priorities, and sequence to what it contains. We use clocks and calendars to measure off certain segments of time: minutes, hours, days; we accept by common consent that one minute as measured by a good clock is the same length as another. In this sense time is essentially static: change is something that takes place within it, but which is not part of its nature. Again, this kind of time is impersonal; its reality derives from a social agreement, not from a personal sensation. If a man dies, 'objective' time continues.

The second aspect of time is the personal experience of it, the ② dynamic process of change and becoming. Time is the journey, not the road. Its pace can vary according to one's mood, emotions, circumstances, and whether one is in a state of anticipation or contentment. It is not measurable; it is composed, not of static temporal relationships such as 'before', 'after', 'earlier', 'later', but of highly relative and changeable ones such as 'past', 'present', and 'future', whose meaning depends entirely on one's own subjective viewpoint. (What is 'past' to us can be 'present' to a man living during the Napoleonic wars and again 'future' to an Elizabethan.) 'Subjective' time ceases for a man when he dies.

These paired viewpoints occur together and in opposition to

each other in some of the plays; for instance, in *As You Like It* and *Romeo and Juliet*. In fact there is considerable moral importance in the choice of which viewpoint one adopts at a given time. It may be not only inappropriate but immoral to take the objective standpoint on time when one is in the arms of one's beloved, to decide, say, how long a kiss will last by the clock, or to see one's friendship as taking up three hours on Mondays, Wednesdays, and Fridays. Alternatively, a statesman who subjectively decided that time would cease when he died, and committed his nation to a disastrous course of action whose consequences he would not live to see, would also be committing an immoral act.

The third aspect of time which appears in this study is time as an agent: time the creator or destroyer, time as the nurse of growth or the architect of decay. Father Time with his scythe is the conventional Renaissance symbol of the latter, though he often had different guises and other significance. The destructive effects of time are not confined to physical objects; they can also produce oblivion and forgetfulness in human memory.

Fourthly, there is time seen as a realm or sphere: the secular or temporal, as opposed to and transcended by the eternal. Plato, St. Augustine, and Boethius are familiar exponents of this concept. It has been one of the great themes of Christian literature in England, from the Anglo-Saxon *Seafarer*, through *The Knight's Tale*, to *Four Quartets*.

The fifth aspect of time which appears here is 'natural' time. The natural world possesses its own cycles, rhythms, and periods: the alternation of day and night, the turning of the seasons, the life cycles of animals and plants. Time in this sense is not, indeed, divorced from the human experience of it: inasmuch as man is an animal, and possesses his own metabolic and growth cycles, and again, inasmuch as he bases his existence on a harmony with seasonal and diurnal changes, he is subject to 'natural' time. The zodiacal signs associated with the emblematic figure of time in many representations are a reference to this aspect of time.

Sixthly, there is time as the medium of cause and effect. Indeed, cause and effect generate the direction of time, and from a purely physical point of view, can be seen as constituting time itself. The temporal world is where fate operates: time may become a tyranny of determinism, a negation of human freedom; or again, it may be sanctified by providence, ordered by benign eternal powers.

⑦ A seventh aspect of time is that of particular moments or periods of time. We say 'the time is ripe' for some action; we talk about 'the right time' and 'the wrong time'; a certain time may be appropriate for one act or word or mood, and not for another. The emblematic figure of 'Occasion', who often merged with Father Time himself, and who was usually represented with a forelock of hair which could be proverbially grasped by an opportunist, was a Renaissance illustration of this sense of the word.

Another emblem showed time unveiling a young woman, who might variously represent truth, deceit, or even luxury (as in the famous *Allegory* of Bronzino in the National Gallery). This illustrates my eighth sense of time, time as revealer or unfolder. Time brings hidden things to light and transforms potentiality into actuality. This effect of time is shown clearly in *The Winter's Tale*, as I shall point out.

Finally, there is time as rhythm: we find this sense in such phrases as 'keeping time', 'musical time'. One man may be out of harmony with another because they have different rhythms of life; or again, a man's personal rhythm may not match with the rhythms of society or of nature. 'Timing', a proper adaptation to the rhythm of a given situation, or perhaps, more subtly, a syncopation with the beat of circumstances, is, as we know, very important in human affairs.

(In this study I shall also be concerned peripherally with plot time in drama, but this is a critical, not a philosophical, category.)

Such a system of classification should be used as a framework to aid clarity of thought, not as a schema into which one seeks to force the actual literary material. When Shakespeare uses the word 'time', or discusses its nature in image or statement, he may be referring to two or more of its aspects at once; or rather, he is dealing with the reality, and not with the intellectual constructs with which *we* attempt to organize it; *his* principles of organization are poetic and dramatic, not necessarily philosophical.

N.B. An Appendix containing passages from some of the writings on time to which Shakespeare might have had direct or indirect access will be found at the end of this book.

2. Time the 'Destroyer' in the Sonnets

IT is, perhaps, dangerous to ascribe a philosophy or a conceptual view of time to the sonnets. J. B. Leishman, in his *Themes and Variations in Shakespeare's Sonnets* (1961), makes an instructive contrast between the intellectual and even speculative tone of Michelangelo's sonnets and the more metaphorical and imagistic tone of Shakespeare's. Shakespeare did consider the nature of the world we live in; but he saw abstract ideas in concrete terms, and for him stones and animals and trees were incarnate thoughts and feelings.

If, then, we are to pursue Shakespeare's ideas about time, we must do it largely through the images he uses. Shakespeare thinks in symbols and in emotional and moral intuitions. He tests an idea not by its internal logical coherence but rather by its appeal to his imagination, his heart, and his moral sense; and by its applicability in a real situation or a concrete image. Often the different contexts and uses of an image will point out to us the associations of ideas that Shakespeare is forming within it. If, for instance, the image of ruins is associated in one poem with the poet's old age, and in another with the decay of the most durable structure by the agency of time, we can infer that Shakespeare associates the loss of youth and physical beauty with the breakdown of order and structure occasioned by the decay of time. A simple example; but we will find whole arguments in the sonnets conducted in terms of the permutations of a single image, like, for instance, the flower–canker–scent–distillation image. Many of these images recur in the plays, and an understanding of their use in the sonnets can help us to perceive their moral colour and relevance there.

In the sonnets as a whole, there are two great themes: love and time. Love is associated by Shakespeare with all that is warmest and most physically present in life: that sense of the living touch of reality which is celebrated in *Venus and Adonis*, the dearness of the relationship of Lear and Cordelia at the end of the play, the warmth of romantic love at the end of the *Merchant of Venice*. Time is the great enemy of all these beautiful and especial things; it seems to question their validity or to give a pessimistic answer to the questions they raise.

Time is a destroyer. It not only carries us towards the end of our lives, but destroys us in every moment. We die in 'every moment', as T. S. Eliot puts it.[1] In Sonnet 60 Shakespeare sees in one sweep all of man's life from birth to death, and identifies the *process* of time with death. The passing of the minutes is part of the whole system of death in which time involves us:

> Like as the waves make towards the pebbled shore,
> So do our minutes hasten to their end;
> Each changing place with that which goes before,
> In sequent toil all forwards do contend. . . .
> . . . Time doth transfix the flourish set on youth,
> And delves the parallels in beauty's brow,
> Feeds on the rarities of nature's truth,
> And nothing stands but for his scythe to mow . . .[2]

Philosophically there is a profound sense in which we are not the same individual as we were a year or even a moment ago: something in us has died. We do not possess that instantaneous and eternal consistency which is ascribed to God or the angels; we are almost a succession of entities, each giving way to its successor, ended by only the last death of many. Death itself is not a single event at the end of a life, but a continuous process.

Time destroys the order and coherence of things, even the most firmly founded:

> When I have seen by Time's fell hand defaced
> The rich proud cost of outworn buried age;
> When sometime lofty towers I see down-rased,
> And brass eternal slave to mortal rage;
> When I have seen the hungry ocean gain
> Advantage on the kingdom of the shore,
> And the firm soil win of the wat'ry main,
> Increasing store with loss, and loss with store;

---

[1] *The Dry Salvages*, l. 159.   [2] Sonnet 60.

> When I have seen such interchange of state,
> Or state itself confounded to decay;
> Ruin hath taught me thus to ruminate—
> That Time will come and take my love away.[3]

Shakespeare looks at material things, however durable or however constructed with craft and skill to defy the ravages of time, and perceives that nevertheless they fall and decay. There is in this sonnet a curious acceleration of the destructive processes of time, which makes the cliffs and towers seem to crumble in a moment—a mockery of their seeming strength! In a thousand years even enduring stone will crumble; how much swifter will be the decay of human beauty and the ending of human life.

In this sonnet is expressed the flux of time, and the very sound and rhythm of the perpetual change and destruction of the sea-coast is evoked: 'Increasing store with loss and loss with store'. The waves seem to beat against the rocks and retreat again and again. (A similar effect is gained in Gerard Manley Hopkins's poem 'The Sea and the Skylark': 'Low lull off, and all roar'.) This is the same coast as that of T. S. Eliot's 'The Dry Salvages', one feels, an ocean equally inimical to the especial and unique beauty of transient things. To 'destroy' means literally to 'unstructure': time attacks order and form. Time's glory in *The Rape of Lucrece* is

> To ruinate proud buildings with thy hours,
> And smear with dust their glitt'ring golden tow'rs;
>
> To fill with worm-holes stately monuments,
> To feed oblivion with decay of things,
> To blot old books and alter their contents . . .[4]

Time attacks identity itself:

> Or state itself confounded to decay.[5]

Here 'state' means not only the pomp and dignity of high position or great riches, but also echoes the meaning of the same word in the previous line: a concept as basic as 'form', 'existence', or 'identity'—the grid-lines of creation itself.

---

[3] Sonnet 64.   [4] *The Rape of Lucrece*, ll 944 et seq.
[5] Sonnet 64.

The process of decay which gives time its direction is evoked in various different images in the sonnets. Sometimes, as in the quotation from *Lucrece*, it is shown in the most homely images of all. If we are not always at work maintaining, tidying, and repairing the ordered and formed things we need about us to keep us alive, they will revert to filth and chaos. If we do not sweep a room, it becomes less of a dwelling-place; wood or iron unpainted rots or rusts; at all times disorder creeps up on us:

> ... And smear with dust their glitt'ring golden tow'rs;
> To fill with worm-holes stately monuments ...

> ... unswept stone, besmear'd with sluttish time.[6]

The image that occurs again and again, as if its associations were so heart-breaking and inexhaustible that Shakespeare could not let it go, is the image of the dying flower:

> Rough winds do shake the darling buds of May,
> And summer's lease hath all too short a date: ...
> ... And every fair from fair sometime declines,
> By chance, or nature's changing course, untrimm'd.[7]

> ... That thereby beauty's rose might never die ...[8]

> How with this rage shall beauty hold a plea,
> Whose action is no stronger than a flower?[9]

In this last quotation the word 'action' keeps its legal sense, but it contains also the simpler and sublime sense of 'power of action'. A flower has no strength at all, and the pathos of this total powerlessness when pitted against the brutal 'rage' of time is enormously effective. The image appeals to our muscle-memories of weakness and to the sense of paralysis we sometimes feel in dreams.

The effectiveness of the flower image used in this way lies largely in the fact that flowers are among the most delicately ordered and intricately formed of creations; they exemplify beauty: but they are at the same time the most fragile of natural objects. If the massive and stubborn order even of works of

---

[6] Sonnet 55.   [7] Sonnet 18.
[8] Sonnet 1.   [9] Sonnet 65.

masonry falls into decay, what chance has the transient order which alone sustains the most intense and sweetest beauty? Time seems to attack order in particular; and it is order from which we get our values and in which we see the possibility of a world untouched by death.

A modern term for the destructive force of time might be the 'increase of entropy'. From a scientific point of view, the process of time can be more or less identified with the increase of entropy, or disorder, in the universe. Shakespeare's intuition of time as increasing disorder and perpetual interchange of state seems oddly echoed by the results of the laboratory. (Yet Herakleitos had come to similar conclusions: 'Fire lives in the death of earth, air in the death of fire, water in the death of air, and earth in the death of water.')[10]

Shakespeare looks at his young friend and at his own youth and sees the forces arrayed against them:

> Against my love shall be as I am now,
> With Time's injurious hand crush'd and o'erworn.[11]

In the Renaissance, when life was shorter and youth more fleeting than they are today, the ideal of beauty was a far younger one. At sixteen one was at the height of beauty; by twenty-five one was middle-aged. Youth is indeed like a flower: the body functions as it should, decrepitude has not yet set in, and the flesh seems for once in life to be a true expression of Man's spirit. Like a flower, youth is a promise; like a promise, it is sometimes sweeter than its fulfilment.

Time is a 'tyrant'[12] who destroys all that he rules over; what are the limits of his dominion? Time's assault is perhaps only on external things. Here social externals are shown to be transient:

> Great princes' favourites their fair leaves spread
> But as the marigold at the sun's eye;
> And in themselves their pride lies buried,
> For at a frown they in their glory die.[13]

[10] Fragment 34; Fragments 28, 29, 40, and 72 are also of interest here.
[11] Sonnet 63.   [12] Sonnet 16.
[13] Sonnet 25.

> If my dear love were but the child of state,
> It might for Fortune's bastard be unfather'd,
> As subject to Time's love or to Time's hate,
> Weeds among weeds, or flowers with flowers gather'd.[14]

Fortune can swiftly disown any emotion based on merely superficial considerations, since such an emotion lays itself open not only to the favour of the temporal but also to its enmity. In Sonnet 125 this subjection of externals to the destructive forces of time is stated clearly:

> Were't aught to me I bore the canopy,
> With my extern the outward honouring,
> Or laid great bases for eternity,
> Which proves more short than waste or ruining?[15]

As in *Love's Labour's Lost*, external rhetoric is opposed to internal feeling:

> ... yet when they have devis'd
> What strained touches rhetoric can lend,
> Thou truly fair wert truly sympathiz'd
> In true plain words by thy true-telling friend ...[16]

> I never saw that you did painting need,
> And therefore to your fair no painting set ...
> ... For I impair not beauty, being mute,
> When others would give life, and bring a tomb.
> There lives more life in one of your fair eyes
> Than both your poets can in praise devise.[17]

Here again it is the externals that bring death, and are involved with death.

This contrast between external, physical things (which pass away) and internal, spiritual things (which can perhaps endure) is very important in the sonnets. We see it stated most effectively, perhaps, in the great flower–scent–distillate image. The external show of beauty is doomed unless it is accompanied by an inner wholesomeness: the internally cankered rose has no perfume, and thus, no hope of continuance:

[14] Sonnet 124.   [15] Sonnet 125.
[16] Sonnet 82.   [17] Sonnet 83.

> The rose looks fair, but fairer we it deem
> For that sweet odour which doth in it live.
> The canker-blooms have full as deep a dye
> As the perfumed tincture of the roses,
> Hang on such thorns, and play as wantonly
> When summer's breath their masked buds discloses;
> But for their virtue only is their show,
> They live unwoo'd, and unrespected fade;
> Die to themselves. Sweet roses do not so:
> Of their sweet deaths are sweetest odours made.[18]

But here a new problem arises; the image of the canker cannot be made to signify anything but the idea of sin. Shakespeare's vision of the destructive effects of time has become an ethic. The moral tone of these lines is unmistakable:

> Ah! wherefore with infection should he live
> And with his presence grace impiety...?
> ...Why should false painting imitate his cheek,
> And steal dead seeming of his living hue?[19]

Sin is marked by a subordination of the inner self to the external world, and to those externals by which the inner self is expressed. Here is a compelling and gruesome image of this:

> ...Before the golden tresses of the dead,
> The right of sepulchres, were shorn away
> To live a second life on second head,
> Ere beauty's dead fleece made another gay.[20]

Sin seeks out dead things to be its expression. There is a curious appropriateness about this: the wages of sin is death. Sin is the rank smell of flowers that have become internally rotten and dead, and have lost their fragrance, their spiritual essence:

> Then, churls, their thoughts, although their eyes were kind,
> To thy fair flower add the rank smell of weeds.
> But why thy odour matcheth not thy show,
> The soil is this—that thou dost common grow.[21]

> ...For canker vice the sweetest buds doth love...[22]

> ...Lilies that fester smell far worse than weeds.[23]

Shakespeare's approach to sin, then, is twofold. Sin can originate

[18] Sonnet 54.   [19] Sonnet 67.   [20] Sonnet 68.
[21] Sonnet 69.   [22] Sonnet 70.   [23] Sonnet 94.

in an involvement of the inner self with its external show; and it becomes in corollary an inner corruption or infection masked by a fair exterior. The soul, in loving dead externals, becomes dead in turn. Sin inverts the proper precedence of human personality, in that it reverses the dependence of outward expression on the inner spirit. For Shakespeare the worst sin is hypocrisy, as we can see clearly in *Hamlet, Lear,* and *Othello.* Beauty, which is noble as the expression of inner worth, becomes the mask of the hypocrite alike in the sonnets and in these plays. In modern psychology there is an interesting analogy with Shakespeare's diagnosis of human evil: the attribution of many of the illnesses of personality to a similar discrepancy between the external *persona* of an individual, and his inner ego. Moreover, when the spirit of a man becomes subordinate to his social or physical self, it comes under the deterministic rules of temporality.

If all that is important in an event or action is its past and future, how can we say that it is not determined, that it is not merely caused by its past and a cause of its future? Within the world of time, the cause–effect relationship is all-powerful: there would be no law in the universe if this were not so. But we can say also that within this world there can be no qualitative judgements, only quantitative ones, for we cannot give value to something which is solely a link in a causal chain. Our feeling of value can apply only to things which are in some way ultimate, which are uncaused, or related to the purpose or end of all existence. Cause denies purpose and intrinsic worth, just as in human affairs it denies responsibility. The bitter pathos in the dying-flower image lay in the fact that Shakespeare saw value and purpose in something which he could not consider at that time as anything but subject to the laws of time. The tragedy of beauty and love is that they demand of us imperatively a recognition and belief in their ultimate value and purpose, but that they exist within the world of time, seemingly ruled over by an unalterable determinism.

It is obvious that if the apparently inexorable laws of entropy and determination have the ultimate sway in the lives of men, we face an existence which is insupportable to our spiritual and moral instincts. We have already seen how in the sonnets the decay of things offends our sense of the everlastingness of that which is beautiful. But time is not only the destroyer of the physical order as we find it in beautiful things; it is also the destroyer of the moral order in Man, if he succumbs to its tyranny. Time the corrupter of the flesh is also the corrupter of the soul. It corrupts us if we involve ourselves with externals, with the world of social favour and outward show that is subject to time. And if we are only creatures of time, then we are governed in our every action by an irreversible deterministic process.

The love that is rooted in appetency is subject to time's laws, and is ended by the bitterness of satiety or forgetfulness. The tragedy of *Troilus and Cressida* is precisely that sensual love is created but also destroyed by time;[24] this feeling is strong also in the sonnets:

> Sweet love, renew thy force; be it not said
> Thy edge should blunter be than appetite . . .[25]

Here the tone is comparatively lighthearted; but the implication that love is limited by time underlies it, and the same image of bluntness is used in Sonnet 95 with the gravest ethical overtones. The last line, which concludes a poem about evil hiding itself beneath a fair outward appearance, is full of foreboding:

> The hardest knife ill-us'd doth lose his edge.

In the following lines, we see in the starkest terms the determinism of lust, which destroys the infinitude of the spirit by a temporal craving or compulsion:

> Th' expense of spirit in a waste of shame
> Is lust in action; and till action, lust
> Is perjur'd, murd'rous, bloody, full of blame,
> Savage, extreme, rude, cruel, not to trust;
> Enjoy'd no sooner but despised straight;
> Past reason hunted, and, no sooner had,
> Past reason hated, as a swallowed bait,
> On purpose laid to make the taker mad—
> Mad in pursuit, and in possession so;
> Had, having, and in quest to have, extreme . . .[26]

[24] See also *Hamlet*, IV, vii 110-23 and my note on these lines on pp. 92–93.
[25] Sonnet 36.   [26] Sonnet 129.

Here the present moment, wherein lies our only hope of freedom from time, becomes only the intermediary stage in a causal sequence between desire and satiety. This terrible bondage is occasioned by a relatively voluntary surrender to the temporal process of cause and effect. The lines themselves seem to follow each other with an inevitable momentum, the repetitions emphasizing the irresistible current of craving.

The flesh itself, then, is one of the externals which must not be allowed to rule over the inner spirit. Physical love must be the external expression of a deeper spiritual movement, if it is not to destroy our freedom. Lust is a fever which perpetuates and increases itself at the price of the individual's free will:

> My love is as a fever, longing still
> For that which longer nurseth the disease;
> Feeding on that which doth preserve the ill,
> Th' uncertain sickly appetite to please.[27]

In Shakespeare the themes of external show and inner reality are often paired with and balanced by the ideas of spiritual blindness and spiritual sight. If the eye is deceived as to the true nature of what it perceives, this can be the result either of the deception of appearances or of some deficiency in perception. In the sonnets time rules autocratically over all false outward appearances; similarly, time is the falsifier of true vision, the deceiver of true sight:

> Thy registers and thee I both defy,
> Not wond'ring at the present nor the past,
> For thy records and what we see doth lie,
> Made more or less by thy continual haste.[28]

> Ah, yet doth beauty, like a dial-hand,
> Steal from his figure, and no pace perceiv'd;
> So your sweet hue, which methinks still doth stand,
> Hath motion, and mine eye may be deceiv'd ...[29]

It is the 'dwellers on form and favour', those who live the materialistic and expedient life of external appearance, whose senses are corrupted, who, for 'compound sweet' forgo 'simple

[27] Sonnet 147.   [28] Sonnet 123.   [29] Sonnet 104.

savour'; whose 'oblation' is therefore 'mix'd with seconds'.[30] This image of impurity in sense impressions has a curious power; when our senses are perverted we cannot taste the refreshment of reality. Touchstone in *As You Like It* satirizes the tastes of the court, which prizes the 'most uncleanly flux of a cat' as a perfume, and whose very perceptions are based on a false scale of values and a retreat from reality into external show.

The love that is based on appetency imposes a temporal tyranny not only on the soul, but also on the sense. Or rather, since it is the soul's business to apprehend reality through the senses, a sick soul cannot have healthy perceptions:[31]

> My love is as a fever, longing still . . .
> . . . Th' uncertain sickly appetite to please.[32]

> O me, what eyes hath Love put in my head,
> Which have no correspondence with true sight![33]

> In faith, I do not love thee with mine eyes,
> For they in thee a thousand errors note.
> But 'tis my heart that loves what they despise,
> Who in despite of view is pleas'd to dote.
> Nor are mine ears with thy tongue's tune delighted;
> Nor tender feeling to base touches prone,
> Nor taste nor smell desire to be invited
> To any sensual feast with thee alone;
> But my five wits nor my five senses can
> Dissuade one foolish heart from serving thee . . .[34]

> O cunning Love! with tears thou keep'st me blind,
> Lest eyes well seeing thy foul faults should find.[35]

Lust presents us with the paradox that the sensual life once chosen does not open but closes the gates of perception. A surrender to sense destroys sense. Sense in Gertrude is 'apoplex'd';[36] the bait of lust makes the taker mad. The determinism

---

[30] Sonnet 125.
[31] 'The light of the body is the eye: if therefore thine eye be single, thy whole body shall be full of light. But if thine eye be evil, thy whole body shall be full of darkness. If therefore the light that is in thee be darkness, how great is that darkness!' Matt. 6: 22–3 (Authorized Version).   [32] Sonnet 147.
[33] Sonnet 148.   [34] Sonnet 141   [35] Sonnet 148.
[36] *Hamlet*, III. iv. 73.

which is imposed by time on the will when it surrenders to temporal things, is extended in the most sinister way to the senses—the only possible instruments of a true perception of reality, and consequently of a cure.

Shakespeare's idea of time, then, has developed from a vision of time as the destroyer of order and beauty, through the conception of time as the ruler of all external and material things, towards an ethic in which time becomes the corrupter of the soul and the senses when human beings yield to the domination of its determinism. All these effects of time seem to aim a destructive blow at love: for love is nourished by beauty, which time destroys; love expresses itself in external and material ways; love is wedded to sensual pleasure; and love demands freedom and a sense of value, neither of which seems to be permitted by the necessity of temporal existence.

How does Shakespeare solve these problems? The first, simplest, and most inadequate answer is the possibility of reproduction. A scientist would say that the living cell is the only thing in nature capable of resisting, by means of resources within itself, the effects of the process of increasing entropy. Life has, in fact, been defined in this way. Life builds and orders; records the past, reproduces itself for the future; and is Shakespeare's first answer to the problems of time. What is today a biological formula Shakespeare would have seen in terms of the resemblance of child to parent, the wonder of an old man at his child's youth and vigour, and the faint sense of immortality we feel at having reproduced our own life in another generation. If the especial beauty of his friend is forever doomed, it may at least be partially and imperfectly transmitted to the future through his children:

This were to be new made when thou art old,
And see the blood warm when thou feel'st it cold[73]

The major image for this in the Sonnets is that of the distilled perfume of a flower. Though the flower dies, the distillate, the seed, the 'D.N.A.', as it were, perpetuates the beauty that must pass:

[37] Sonnet 2.

> From fairest creatures we desire increase,
> That thereby beauty's rose might never die . . .[38]

> Then, were not summer's distillation left
> A liquid prisoner pent in walls of glass,
> Beauty's effect with beauty were bereft,
> Nor it, nor no remembrance what it was;
> But flowers distill'd, though they with winter meet,
> Leese but their show; their substance still lives sweet.[39]

Again we see the contrast between the external accidents of beauty, which are transient, and the inner essence which may survive.

The cycle of the seasons is another image which Shakespeare uses when he pits the power of physical life and reproduction against the power of time. The distillate that is preserved is the distillation of summer which can resist the ravages of winter and become the seed of a new spring.

But Shakespeare was dissatisfied with this merely cyclic reproduction of lost beauty. There is something so especial about his friend's beauty, so archetypal, that once it has gone, it is as if the essence of beauty itself were destroyed, as if nature had cracked the mould: 'Thy end is truth's and beauty's doom and date'.[40] In Sonnet 53 all forms of beauty are only Platonic shadows of his substance. No genetic replica can do justice to its original. That uniqueness which gives beauty its character is welded to all that is most temporal and transient in it. Shakespeare faces T. S. Eliot's problem:

> Time and the bell have buried the day
> The black cloud carries the sun away.
> Will the sunflower turn to us; will the clematis
> Stray down, bend us; tendril and spray
> Clutch and cling?[41]

Although, says Eliot, we may find a way to the 'stillness that is the dance' by means of rejection and darkness, there is still the problem of what happens to the transient beauty that we feel to be valid. That the cycle of the seasons will bring another spring is

[38] Sonnet 1.   [39] Sonnet 5.
[40] Sonnet 14.   [41] *Burnt Norton*, l. 127.

not enough. There is something especial and particular that must, it seems, pass away. Shakespeare must search for another answer to the problem of beauty's transience. In Sonnet 19 he accepts that time will devour his friend's beauty; it is in desperation that he defies time with his poetry, admitting that beauty will pass, but asserting that something can be rescued from its wreck:

> But I forbid thee one most heinous crime:
> O, carve not with thy hours my love's fair brow,
> Nor draw no lines there with thine antique pen;
> Him in thy course untainted do allow
> For beauty's pattern to succeeding men.
> Yet, do thy worst, old Time. Despite thy wrong,
> My love shall in my verse ever live young.[42]

The word 'love' in this last line is perhaps ambiguous: it could refer not only to Shakespeare's friend but also to his own feeling of love. If the ambiguity is there, then we can infer that Shakespeare is groping towards a conception of beauty as the effect of love, which can be preserved, where beauty cannot. The argument might in this case go thus: 'Time can indeed irrecoverably destroy those physical externals which love invests with beauty: but in order to destroy the inner essence of beauty, which is the love we feel for what we call beautiful, time must destroy the love that gave it beauty: but this love is preserved in verse.' In Sonnet 130 Shakespeare, because of his love for her, finds beauty in a woman who appears to have no justification for being called beautiful. If human beauty is no more than the effect of the loved one on the lover, it can perhaps be preserved by recording the love that produced it.

The pathos of beauty was that it was external, and thus subject to time; and that it was a delicate order, and time's most savage assault was on order. But poetry is an imperishable order, in contrast with all the structures of Man's hand or nature's, and is independent of the physical means of its expression.

The image of distilled perfume is used also in this, the second of Shakespeare's answers to the problem of time:

[42] Sonnet 19.

> ... Sweet roses do not so:
> Of their sweet deaths are sweetest odours made.
> And so of you, beauteous and lovely youth,
> When that shall vade, by verse distills your truth.[43]

The inner spirit, 'truth' (or, as often, 'worth') is preserved by poetry. A kind of immortality is promised, though it is the immortality only of the essence, not the accidents of beauty:

> Gainst death and all-oblivious[44] enmity
> Shall you pace forth; your praise shall still find room
> Even in the eyes of all posterity
> That wear this world out to the ending doom.[45]

Even poetry can last only as long as the earth endures. But with that objection poetry is as good a way as any of preserving something of one's personal identity:

> The earth can have but earth, which is his due;
> My spirit is thine, the better part of me.
> So then thou hast but lost the dregs of life,
> The prey of worms, my body being dead;
> The coward conquest of a wretch's knife,
> Too base of thee to be remembered.
> The worth of that is that which it contains,
> And that is this, and this with thee remains.[46]

These sonnets do not just describe the fear that Shakespeare's friend must lose his youth: there is also an undercurrent of terror at his own personal extinction, and, worse still, a foreboding that perhaps that love which the poet feels and celebrates will itself fade away. Why else does Shakespeare dwell not only on the possibility of his friend's death, but also on the disappearance of those charms that compel his love? Indeed, if we accept the suggestion that beauty was to Shakespeare the externalization of love, then the vanishing of beauty would naturally imply the disappearance of love. In a sense, 'every poem' is 'an epitaph';[47] each of these poems celebrates and attempts to eternalize a state

---

[43] Sonnet 54.
[44] I am unhappy about Alexander's hyphenation here. Surely Shakespeare means 'all things which are hostile in that they forget' rather than 'enmity that forgets everything'.
[45] Sonnet 55.   [46] Sonnet 74.   [47] 'Little Gidding', l. 225.

of mind and soul that may pass away. And here, ultimately, the power of poetry is an inadequate answer to the problem of time. Poetry can only preserve beauty when it is informed by love; but poetry does not guarantee the endurance of love itself. We have seen the traps which time lays for the lover: the snare of super-ficiality, the pitfall of appetency, the prison of behavioural deter-minism. Poetry merely extends the memory of love (and hence the beauty projected by love on what is loved) in time: it is only a recording, not the perpetuation of an entity. Shakespeare had recognized in the early sonnets that 'barren rime' was second-best; at best, a second-hand version of reality. What he is looking for is a vision of love which is eternally valid in itself, which tri-umphs over time not just by being recorded, but by being inde-pendent of time. Poetry is an attempt to internalize external beauty, to give it a reinforcement of form and order which it does not already possess, so that it may endure in time. Shakespeare's final answer is that true beauty *is* internal, that true beauty is generated by a kind of love to which time is irrelevant: in the modern phrase, timeless.

Shakespeare is one of the creators of the modern ideal of love. In him Platonic love, courtly love, the Christian idea of Charity, that is, moral love, and a new aesthetic kind of love came together. It was a synthesis novel to the age, a unique product of the Renaissance.

The Shakespearean lover sees his beloved as the archetype of beauty, and worships him like a divine being. Not 'worship' as the courtly lovers would have meant it; but in the sense that we feel sometimes when we have seen something in another person to which we could go down on our knees. Beyond this, almost for the first time in history, love is here a relationship, something that is distinct from the individuals involved and which is greater than the sum of its parts: something that resolves the unbearable separateness of the closest lovers. This ecstatic love is celebrated in 'The Phoenix and the Turtle'.

Love of this kind was a novel and marvellous discovery, a view of the world with new eyes, a complete reshuffling of the priorities of motive and desire. Donne calls his mistress his 'New-Found

Land';[48] it is perhaps fitting that while the terrestrial globe was being explored and suddenly illuminated, new areas of the human experience of personal relationship were similarly being opened up. To worship another person was not bathetic, as it sometimes appears today, but a daring leap into a new mode of experience: the worship of a person for his own sake; the desire, not for pleasure or gain, but for the good of the beloved; the rejection, finally, of anything in oneself that is unworthy of participation in that relationship.

Shakespeare meant his sonnets for 'lovers' eyes',[49] we must remember, and, if we do not approach them as lovers, who are quite at home among wild hyperboles, they will seem over-done, exaggerated, and cloying. We must be prepared to accept the I–thou relationship which we find there, in as humble and as proud a spirit as Shakespeare's own.

It is a love which harnesses all man's spiritual energies that Shakespeare finally opposes to the destructive and corrupting forces of time. A love which is not dependent on externals, which transcends the laws of cause and effect, and which even, perhaps, generates the only genuine beauty.

Love, in the following lines, is seen as resurrecting the past which has been destroyed by time, and making 'what might have been' present:

> But if the while I think on thee, dear friend,
> All losses are restor'd, and sorrows end.[50]

> Thou art the grave where buried love doth live,
> Hung with the trophies of my lovers gone,
> Who all their parts of me to thee did give;
> That due of many now is thine alone.
> Their images I lov'd I view in thee,
> And thou, all they, hast all the all of me.[51]

Love is the only force that can internalize and make valid the transient external beauty which is so subject to time's destruction:

[48] 'To his Mistris Going to Bed', l. 27.
[50] Sonnet 30.
[49] Sonnet 55.
[51] Sonnet 31.

So that eternal love in love's fresh case
Weighs not the dust and injury of age,
Nor gives to necessary wrinkles place,
But makes antiquity for aye his page;
Finding the first conceit of love there bred,
Where time and outward form would show it dead.[52]

Beauty is hardly important any more: it is only the outward show
of something that can exist without it, or alternatively only the
effect on the senses of what is loved:

In him those holy antique hours are seen,
Without all ornament, itself and true,
Making no summer of another's green,
Robbing no old to dress his beauty new ...[53]

'Itself and true' is an almost existentialist formulation of the
curious frankness and lucidity that the reality of a loved person
seems to possess. What astounds the true lover, perhaps, is that
he feels that for the first time he is in the unclouded presence of
a reality outside himself, that what he sees is no longer falsified
by the separation that exists between the self and all other things.
At one blow this new concept of love has swept away the enemies
of love—determinism, superficiality and deception; for this love
is a going outside oneself, a renunciation of self-will and even of
one's own personality. Once we are beyond our own self and our
own will, we are beyond the killing touch of our own deterministic motives and temporal cravings: in a state perhaps akin
to the Buddhist act of contemplation, where the soul attains freedom from the world of sensation and illusion. Love in this sense
frees us from the vicious circle of time:

If my dear love were but the child of State,
It might for Fortune's bastard be unfather'd
As subject to Time's love or to Time's hate,
Weeds among weeds, or flowers with flowers gather'd.
No, it was builded far from Accident;
It suffers not in smiling Pomp, nor falls
Under the blow of thralled Discontent,
Whereto th' inviting time our fashion calls.

[52] Sonnet 108.   [53] Sonnet 68.

It fears not Policy, that heretic,
Which works on leases of short-numb'red hours,
But all alone stands hugely politic,
That it nor grows with heat nor drowns with show'rs.
To this I witness call the fools of Time
Which die for goodness, who have lived for crime.[54]

I have capitalized 'State', 'Fortune', 'Accident', 'Pomp', 'Discontent', 'Time', as well as 'Policy' in this poem because they are a series of personified abstractions, which are linked in a relentless logic. 'State', that is 'conditions', 'circumstances', or 'the way things are', is ruled over by 'Fortune'; 'Fortune' produces 'Accident' or chance; 'Accident' may give rise to good luck or bad, either 'Pomp' or 'Discontent'. To fight against this system by plots and cunning is to follow 'Policy', the heretic or rebel, which is in any case itself subject to 'leases of short-numb'red hours'. Together these personifications comprise the 'fools of Time', which 'die for goodness' (must cease to exist if there is to be goodness) 'who have lived for crime' (and which generate sin by their presence in the human heart). They are the 'fools of Time' because they are all subject to time, as the poet takes pains to point out. Shakespeare summons to give witness against themselves the very forces that can weaken love in its lawsuit against time. This reading (which I have not found elsewhere) makes sense of a sonnet that has puzzled its commentators and editors.

In this sonnet love need not fear Policy, that is, the necessities of expedience and the determinism of self-will. It is neither voluntary nor does it tolerate any motive in the lover that is not concerned with the good of the loved one. It is a determinant itself, it has its own will which overrules all petty tyranny of craving and self-interest: it is 'hugely politic'. It is not changed by externals but iself can change the external world.

True love can also open the gates of perception which have been closed by the deceptions of time. The constancy of true love is able to overcome the inconstancy of all temporal perceptions:

Thy registers and thee I both defy,
Not wond'ring at the present nor the past,
For thy records and what we see doth lie,

[54] Sonnet 124.

Made more or less by thy continual haste.
This do I vow, and this shall ever be:
I will be true, despite thy scythe and thee.[55]

Lust is able to gild evil and deceive the honesty of the senses: true love can ignore the merely superficial aspects of perception and penetrate to the reality beneath. Lust is less honest than the evidence of the senses: true love is more honest than sense-perception.

Were't ought to me I bore the canopy,
With my extern the outward honouring,
Or laid great bases for eternity,
Which proves more short than waste or ruining?
Have I not seen dwellers on form and favour
Lose all, and more, by paying too much rent,
For compound sweet forgoing simple savour—
Pitiful thrivers, in their gazing spent?
No, let me be obsequious in thy heart,
And take thou my oblation, poor but free,
Which is not mix'd with seconds, knows no art
But mutual render, only me for thee.[56]

These lines sum up most of what Shakespeare has to say about true love: its inner, personal nature, untainted by temporal externals; its vision, which is 'poor but free', and at first hand, existential, not 'mix'd with seconds'. The gates of true perception are opened by love, so that there is nothing impure or second-hand about it. 'Simple savour' is rightly preferred to 'compound sweet'; that which nourishes is better than that which merely titillates. This is a form of love which is not concerned with gratification but with existence: it makes the lover exist more fully.

Shakespeare eventually accepts the terrible temporal forces that are pitted against what he holds dear. But at the end he realizes that they are irrelevant to love:

Let me not to the marriage of true minds
Admit impediments. Love is not love
Which alters when it alteration finds,
Or bends with the remover to remove.

[55] Sonnet 123.   [56] Sonnet 125.

O, no ! it is an ever-fixed mark,
That looks on tempests and is never shaken;
It is the star to every wand'ring bark,
Whose worth's unknown, although his height be taken.
Love's not Time's fool, though rosy lips and cheeks
Within his bending sickle's compass come;
Love alters not with his brief hours and weeks,
But bears it out even to the edge of doom.
If this be error, and upon me prov'd,
I never writ, nor no man ever lov'd.[57]

Love is not time's fool. All things which are external can be measured; but love's worth cannot be so confined. If we can be certain of anything, Shakespeare asserts, we can be certain of this. He has asked what we can oppose against time's destructive and corrupting forces; he saw that the replications of the flesh and the order of poetry had some strength against its ravages, but his last and only real answer is a relationship.

[57] Sonnet 116.

3. As You Like It: 'Subjective', 'Objective', and 'Natural' Time

As You Like It opens with two characters who, in terms of the hierarchy of social power, are weak and inferior: Orlando, the younger brother, and Adam, the old man. One is denied his place in society; the other is past his usefulness. Orlando tellingly distinguishes between the 'gentle condition of blood' and the 'courtesy of nations';[1] between what is owed him as a member of society, and what is due to his status as a human being. Adam has 'lost' his 'teeth' 'in service',[2] and though his master's legal obligation to him has been fulfilled, Oliver refuses to honour his human obligations to look after the faithful servant in his old age.

Those who are weak in the power structure of society—children, old men, beggars, strangers, the insane—can possess the most potent moral power in the human community. But this moral power must be recognized, if it is to exist; Malvolio's crime, we shall see, is to deny the moral power of the Fool. Orlando's description of his 'keeping' as no different from the 'stalling of an ox',[3] and Oliver's characterizing Adam as an 'old dog',[4] suggest that the socially strong in this play consider those who are socially weak to be no better than beasts, outside the community of man, and therefore ineligible for the basic human rights. But piety (or pité), insists that such figures are the true representatives of the human community, that we should treat them with the respect due to common humanity, whose dignity transcends the evanescent privileges of rank, wealth, or birth. There is only one thing that Orlando and Adam can do: leave the society which has rejected them.

Outcast also are the Duke Senior and his friends, and Rosalind, Celia, and Touchstone. Where can they go? What region of

---

[1] I. i. 40.   [2] I. i. 75.   [3] I. i. 8.   [4] I. i. 73.

Shakespeare's poetic, philosophical, and moral world is appropriate to them?

If one escapes from the ordinary routine of society, one is on holiday. Rosalind can see nothing but 'briers' in this 'working-day' world; on 'holiday' they are but 'burs'. If, says Celia, 'we walk not in the trodden paths'—if we do not conform to the routines of society—'our very petticoats will catch them'.[5] The holiday that the outcasts must take is partly a holiday of the mind. 'Briers' become 'burs' when their attitude changes from 'working-day' to 'holiday'. Rosalind and Celia come to accept their existence with patience, but without paying the price of a vitiating and stoic detachment. On holiday life is only a game, even when it is a game of life and death. Rosalind and Celia are delightful partly because of their holiday attitude to the world—an attitude which combines levity with involvement, wisdom with feeling. Rosalind can satirize love and be in love at the same time.

Orlando, Rosalind, and the Duke Senior are all victims of injustice. They reject and are rejected by the power-structure of their society; and this structure includes its laws. The 'courtesy of nations' has become a tyranny for Orlando; for the Duke Senior it has been overturned. The accusation of treachery levelled by Duke Frederick at Rosalind is a legality divested of its sanctifying ritual of evidence, fair play, and impartiality. Thus the exiles become outlaws: they live 'like the old Robin Hood of England'.[6] This brings to mind the connection of Robin Hood with the old holiday ritual of rural England, and the enormous popularity of his story among the common folk. He was the hero of the socially weak; the semi-pagan god of Holiday. The Puritans recognized this strain in his cult when they abolished it nearly fifty years later.

Time in the forest is not social time. The exiled nobles 'fleet the time carelessly, as they did in the golden world'.[7] They 'lose and neglect the creeping hours of time;[8] the human measurement of time has no meaning here. In Thomas Mann's *Magic Mountain*, holiday has a similar effect:

[5] I. iii. 12 et seq.

[7] I. i. 109

[6] I. i. 106.

[8] II. vii. 112.

Such is the purpose of our changes of air and scene, of all our
sojourns at cures and bathing resorts; it is the secret of the healing
power of change and incident. Our first days in a new place, time has
a youthful, that is to say, a broad and sweeping flow, persisting for
some six or eight days. Then, as one 'gets used to the place', a gradual
shrinkage makes itself felt. He who clings or, better expressed,
wishes to cling to life, will shudder to see how the days grow light
and lighter, how they scurry by like dead leaves, until the last week,
of some four, perhaps, is uncannily fugitive and fleet.[9]

Here Mann is more interested in the subjective changes in the
rate of time occasioned by circumstances than in the nature of
holiday itself; but one interest tends to suggest the other, and we
will find Shakespeare himself fascinated with subjective time
in turn.

Helen Gardner discusses this subject illuminatingly in the
context of the romantic comedies in general: 'In Shakespeare's
comedies time . . . is not so much a movement onward as a space
in which to work things out: a midsummer night, a space too
short for us to feel time's movement, or the unmeasured time of
As You Like It or *Twelfth Night*.'[10] Of *Much Ado About Nothing* she says: 'A sense of holiday, of *time off from the world's
business*, reigns in Messina.'[11]

Twice in *As You Like It* the absurdity of social, measurable
time is suggested:

> And then he drew a dial from his poke,
> And, looking on it with lack-lustre eye,
> Says very wisely 'It is ten o'clock;
> Thus we may see' quoth he 'how the world wags;
> 'Tis but an hour ago since it was nine;
> And after one hour more 'twill be eleven; . . .'
>   . . . When I did hear
> The motley fool thus moral on the time,
> My lungs began to crow like chanticleer

[9] *The Magic Mountain,* ch. iv, 'Excursus on the the Sense of Time', trans. H. T.
Lowe-Porter, New York, 1939.
[10] *As You Like It* by Helen Gardner, from *More Talking about Shakespeare*,
ed. John Garrett, 1959.
[11] Op. cit. My italics.

That fools should be so deep contemplative;
And I did laugh sans intermission
An hour by his dial.[12]

—Is it significant that Jaques compares his laughter to the sound of the chanticleer, the marker of natural time as opposed to the time of clocks?—

Ros: I pray you, what is't o'clock?
Orl: You should ask me what time o'day; there's no clock in the forest.[13]

This last is reminiscent of Falstaff's first words in *I Henry IV*, and Hal's reply:

Fal: Now, Hal, what time of day is it, lad? ... etc.[14]

The Boar's Head is similarly on holiday from ordinary time. It is interesting that what follows in each case is also similar. Rosalind asserts that

'Then there is no true lover in the forest, else sighing every minute and groaning every hour would detect the lazy foot of Time as well as a clock.'[15]

Hal says to Falstaff:

What a devil hast thou to do with the time of the day? Unless hours were cups of sack, and minutes capons, and clocks the tongues of bawds ... etc.[16]

Time in each case is transmuted from the measurable, social time of clocks into the subjective time of experience. Falstaff now introduces another element:

... we that take purses go by the moon and the seven stars, and not by Phoebus, he 'that wand'ring knight so fair'.[17]

Falstaff operates, so he claims, according to the natural and mysterious time of the moon and the stars, rather than the tamed and social time of the sun—which he anthropomorphizes with impunity.

The Forest of Arden is a poetic region which contains, as well as holiday and outlawry, the forces of natural time, the time of the

[12] II. vii. 20 et seq.   [13] III. ii. 282 et seq.   [14] *1 Henry IV*, 1. ii. 1.
[15] III. ii. 285.   [16] *1 Henry IV*, I. ii. 5.   [17] Ibid., I. ii. 12.

seasons, of the great rhythms of nature; 'time not our time',[18] as
T. S. Eliot puts it.

> Under the greenwood tree
> Who loves to lie with me,
> And turn his merry note
> Unto the sweet bird's throat . . .
> . . . Here shall he see
> No enemy
> But winter and rough weather.[19]

> Here feel we but the penalty of Adam,
> The seasons' difference . . .[20]

> Blow, blow, thou winter wind,
> Thou are not so unkind
> As man's ingratitude . . .[21]

Shakespeare's Arden contains other seasons than a perpetual
springtime. It can be 'melancholy',[22] 'uncouth',[23] a 'desert inaccessible';[24] it contains real, as well as conventional, shepherds.
Most important of all, it works convincingly by natural time. It is
a place one lives in, not an abstraction of the poet's mind; it has
the obduracy and unconcern for human desires that we recognize
as authentic in nature. People can get old here in the forest; time
rules over man, but it is the time of the seasons and not the time
of the clock.

The exiles carry with them into the forest many of their
human attitudes and preconceptions. Jaques relentlessly anthropomorphizes the deer; the nobles are seen as 'usurpers' on the life
of the forest, which is contrasted with the human domains of
'country, city, court'.[25] For our purposes one of the most significant importations into the forest is Jaques' attitude to time in
human existence:

> All the world's a stage,
> And all the men and women merely players;

---

[18] 'The Dry Salvages', l. 36.   [19] II. v. 1.
[20] II. i. 5. I prefer 'but' to 'not' here. There is justification for either, though
the Folio has 'not'.
[21] II. vii. 174.   [22] II. vii. 111.   [23] II. vi. 5.
[24] II. vii. 110.   [25] II. i. 59.

They have their exits and their entrances;
And one man in his time plays many parts,
His acts being seven ages . . .
                              . . . Last scene of all,
That ends this strange eventful history,
Is second childishness and mere oblivion;
Sans teeth, sans eyes, sans taste, sans everything.[26]

This passage resembles the conventional picture of the attitude
of the philosopher. Jaques is above it all; he preserves a lofty
detachment from the affairs of the common herd. But his detachment denies to him much of the truth about human existence.
This celebrated passage is oddly hypermetropic: Jaques is
longsighted, and cannot see the trees for the wood. The statistical
studies of sociologists frequently give the same impression of
selective blindness. The individual is devalued, exceptions are
discounted, particulars yield to trends, freedom and significance
are made to seem absurd or irrelevant.

Two elements of this speech are of particular interest: first,
the life of man in time as a stage play; and, second, that life as a
'history', a succession of objectively observable characteristics of
behaviour.

'All the world's a stage.' In a play, the actor is bound to the
lines that the dramatist has written for him. He is not free to say
or do what he likes; man, according to Jaques, is only reading off
a preordained script. A play exists before it is performed; time is
like a motion picture, every frame of which has already been prepared. Life is only the playing-out of a set sequence of events, the
projection of a reel of scenes. Part of the irony of Jaques' speech
is that it is, of course, delivered by an actor who is himself
keeping to his part.

Walter Bagehot makes an interesting point about Jaques'
speech in a passage which David Cecil quotes and discusses in his
charming essay, 'Shakespearean Comedy', from *The Fine Art of
Reading*.[27] Bagehot's treatment deserves repetition:

There seems an unalterable contradiction between the human
mind and its employments How can a soul be a merchant? What

[26] II. vii. 139 et seq.   [27] 1957.

relation to an immortal being have the price of linseed, the fall of butter, the tare on tallow, or the brokerage on hemp? Can an undying creature debit 'petty expenses,' and charge for 'carriage paid'? All the world's a stage;—'the satchel, and the shining morning face' —the 'strange oaths';—'the bubble reputation'— the

> Eyes severe and beard of formal cut,
> Full of wise saws and modern instances.

Can these things be real? Surely they are acting. What relation have they to the truth as we see it in theory? What connection with our certain hopes, 'in respect of itself, it is a good life; but in respect it is a Shepherd's life, it is nought'. The soul ties its shoes; the mind washes its hands in a basin. All is incongruous.

In a play the actors are not being themselves, but donning masks and acting a pretence. Jaques' vision of human life is essentially external. For him all there is is the pretence, the mask, the actor's part, the accidents. He describes behaviour, but not experience. Jaques is, perhaps, the first of those great satirical *personae* that Hugh Kenner discusses with such penetration and wit in his 'historical comedy', *The Counterfeiters*.[28] Like Gulliver describing the Yahoos, like the extraordinary counterfeit sociologist who seems to have written *A Modest Proposal*, like the bad poet Pope invents to write the *Art of Sinking in Poetry*, Jaques is concerned not with the inner nature of a person, but with his surface, not with another 'I' but with an 'it'.

The reader, abetted by many critics, is often deceived in this passage by its breadth, inclusiveness, and metaphysical pathos into feeling that this is Shakespeare's viewpoint on the world, that here is some kind of ultimate wisdom about human life. On the contrary, Jaques' description of the schoolboy, lover, soldier, is only a series of brilliantly evoked stereotypes. If in some respects Shakespeare is *creating* or *originating* stereotypes (like Chaucer in the Prologue to the *Canterbury Tales*), this does not alter the fact that we are not being told the whole story about human existence; the sample of human information Jaques has chosen is not a fair one, and whole areas have been suppressed. Equally as important as what Jaques says is the insight we get

[28] Indiana U.P., 1968.

into Jaques' point of view, and indeed into the flaws and virtues of a whole way of looking at existence.

Jaques' speech contains a certain cynicism, a mood alien, in some respects, to Shakespeare's own, as far as we can judge from his poems and sonnets, as well as from his plays. The other passages we should bear in mind when we read or hear 'All the world's a stage' include not only Prospero's 'our revels now are ended', and 'as an unperfect actor on the stage'; but also Macbeth's 'poor player, That struts and frets his hour upon the stage', and Lear's 'great stage of fools'. Jaques' vision of human life ends as it began: with second childishness, sans everything; nothing has been gained, life is meaningless, it's all only a play. As soon as Jaques has finished his speech, Orlando, the young man and the lover, enters carrying Adam, the old man who is almost in his 'last scene'; the two are united and ennobled by a sense of love and care which somehow transcends and contradicts the stereotypical categories that would divide and degrade them.

The other theme of Jaques' speech that concerns us here is that of man's life as a history. 'History' can have two meanings, both of which are relevant in this context: 'story', and 'history' in the modern sense. The essential element in both is their dialectic: time in both is something expressed in terms of 'before' and 'after' rather than 'past', 'present', and 'future'. Time for 'history' is something static. The most obvious characteristic of Jacques' speech is the way for him human life seems to go in stages, each of which is changeless and restrictingly self-consistent. We can all remember our sense of chagrin and frustration when we were told by our parents that we were 'just going through a stage'. Our individuality, the validity of our ideals and feelings, seemed threatened. When, we asked, would we be real people, when would we cease to be merely the result of a biological or social situation? Jaques would, it seems, reply 'never'.

'His acts being seven ages.' This ignores a fundamental characteristic of time—time as flux, time as dynamic process. Jaques' human actor develops in a curiously jerky fashion. We cannot for the life of us see how that particular kind of lover can become that particular kind of soldier or lawyer. How does the plump

Justice become the 'lean and slipper'd pantaloon'? We have no
sense of this man being one person. In our own lives we can look
back and sometimes fail to recognize what we call 'I'; but
usually beneath the affectations and obsessions, the attempts to be
what we were not, we can see one person whom we greet with
almost the delighted shock of meeting an old friend unexpec-
tedly. There is none of this in Jaques' creed. Yet time is seamless.
It has no stages. And it is in this intimate connection of each
moment of time with the next that the possibility of being one
person, not just an infinite sequence of stages, can exist. If one
takes an individual out of his temporal context at various stages
of his development, as Jaques does, one will inevitably falsify as
well as omit much of what he is.

Jaques sees himself as an 'historian', chronicling the life of
man. Now 'history' in this sense is concerned with events and
states; it cannot afford to occupy itself with the subtle rhythms of
gradual growth. The dialectic of 'historical' time, as I have
pointed out in the Introduction, is based on terms like 'before',
'after', 'earlier', and later', not on 'past', present', and 'future'.
But the rhythm of growth is the rhythm of continuous, impercep-
tible change; and the growing-point of a human life is the
present moment which carries with it the concepts of 'past' and
'future' as indications of the direction of growth. To take temporal cross-sections is to ignore the *process* of growth, concen-
trating only on its effects and results.

'History' in Jaques' sense, moreover, like philosophy, is a map;
a map cannot reproduce the whole landscape in its minute detail.
Yet we can only really know the landscape ('known' as *connaître,*
not *savoir*), if we have all its details about us. A work of art can
give us a sense of this but the pre-rational and personal principles
of selection which are available to the artist are denied to Jaques'
'historian', who is in pursuit of impersonal truth, whose satire
'like a wild-goose flies, Unclaim'd of any man',[29] and who pro-
fesses a disillusioned rationality.

Part of the force of Falstaff, perhaps, is that he is a dynamic
character who changes and evolves in an environment of static,

[29] II. vii. 86.

'historical' time—the time of events and states. Falstaff is a work
of art, and in fact develops from a wildly inaccurate selection and
exaggeration by Shakespeare of meagre details in his sources.

Jaques' 'historical' viewpoint has other characteristics. One is
that it is objective, rather than subjective. Jaques does not take
into account what is almost the most important feature of time—
the peculiar sensation, common to the human race, and therefore
taken for granted, of living in time. What does it feel like to live
in time? Everything that comes under that question is absent
from Jaques' point of view. Since values and meaning exist only
in the subjective sphere,[30] Jaques is presenting a view of existence
as valueless and meaningless. Since the sense of the living self
exists only in the present moment (which is given no particular
significance by Jaques), he is describing people who seem to
have no self.

Jaques describes 'dead time'—time with no present moments.
The advantage the dissector has when working with a dead body
rather than a live one is that there is no change in the material
being dissected: the body can get no deader. The vivisectionist,
on the other hand, has always to beware of the fact that, like
Heisenberg's electrons, his subject will be altered by the process
of observation. Jaques is safe, working with dead time, and indeed
his analytical method is appropriate to his subject. When we
work with live time, however, we will find the present moment
slipping away in an instant, and other methods of comprehension
than Jaques' analytical and objective one must be found.

Finally, we may give attention to Jaques' use of generalization
in this speech. 'In all cases, or at least in a good statistical major-
ity, human beings will act in such and such a way' he seems to
say. To generalize requires an initial comparison, or 'making
equal', of those things about which one generalizes. If I use the
generalizing word 'tree', I am assuming *a priori* that oaks, pines,
elms, palms, etc., are all in some way basically the same. Indeed,
generalization, like the historical dialectic, like objectivity, like

[30] In using the word 'subjective' I am not attempting to undermine values and
meanings; rather I am emphasizing the importance of subjectivity as a way of
perceiving truth, and trying to redefine and revive the stronger senses of the word.

the analytic method of thought itself, is essential in order to come at many kinds of truth. About human beings themselves we can and must generalize to a large extent in order to obtain the most primary understanding. But there seems to be something in every sane, undefeated human being that cries out for uniqueness, peerlessness, a sense of his own incomparability. Again, Jaques is not telling the whole story about human existence.

Both Jaques and Touchstone satirize the extravagant claims of love; but their points of view should not be confused. What Jaques says is 'see how absurd is the lover, with his sighs and ballads; for what is he, when his act is past? What a puny figure he cuts in the perspective of history! Does he not swiftly turn into something quite different? Surely his self-importance is misplaced. He is only a stage between schoolboy and soldier. His transports and agonies have no significance.' What Touchstone says is subtly different: 'What is love but Nature's mechanism for repeopling the earth? When it comes down to it, sex is what the whole thing amounts to after all. I myself, with all my wit, "press in" among the "country copulatives";[31] we are all part of the same natural rhythm, there is no qualitative difference between true lovers and the mating of beasts. The true significance of love is biological; the rest only icing on the cake.' Jaques sees the lover in the perspective of history; Touchstone, against the backdrop of brute nature; Jaques' ultimate reality is death, Touchstone's the natural cycle of reproduction; Jaques questions value, Touchstone's values are materialistic.

Posed against both viewpoints are the attitudes of the lovers. If Jaques in his great speech expresses the 'historical' view of time, Rosalind and Orlando are the representatives of 'personal' time. Time for them is dynamic:

> *Orl*: And why not the swift foot of Time? Had not that been as proper?
> *Ros*: By no means, sir. Time travels in divers paces with divers persons. I'll tell you who Time ambles withal, who Time trots withal, who Time gallops withal, and who he stands still withal.
> *Orl*: I prithee, who doth he trot withal?

[31] v. iv. 54.

Ros: Marry, he trots hard with a young maid between the contract of her marriage and the day it is solemniz'd; if the interim be but a se'nnight, Time's pace is so hard that it seems the length of seven year.

Orl: Who ambles Time withal?

Ros: With a priest that lacks Latin and a rich man that hath not the gout; for the one sleeps easily because he cannot study, and the other lives merrily because he feels no pain; the one lacking the burden of lean and wasteful learning, the other knowing no burden of heavy tedious penury. These Time ambles withal.

Orl: Who doth he gallop withal?

Ros: With a thief to the gallows; for though he go as softly as foot can fall, he thinks himself too soon there.

Orl: Who stays it still withal?

Ros: With lawyers in the vacation; for they sleep between term and term, and they perceive not how Time moves.[32]

| Here time is a pace or journey.| At first glance this dialogue apears fairly simple: a witty expression of the commonplaces contained in such phrases as 'how time drags!' and 'time flies'. But in fact this passage is extravagantly difficult. Surely the conventional way of describing the young maid's suspense would be in terms of the slowness of time. Time 'crawls', we would imagine, for the waiting girl. But for Shakespeare it 'trots'. Why? Perhaps Shakespeare means that, for her, every moment is crowded with emotions, fancies, and anticipations. Clock time inches past; her own personal time is in a furious hurry| A week contains seven years' subjective events. The actual sense of motion is important here. When a horse trots, it throws one about a good deal more than when it gallops. One is not actually progressing as fast as at a gallop, but a half-hour's trot can leave as many unpleasant after-effects as a whole morning's gallop. Shakespeare is talking here as much about the *rhythm* of time as about anything else.|

//With the priest and the rich man the emphasis is different. Time 'ambles' for them because there is little in their lives of excitement, anticipation, or pain: but chiefly because an amble

[32] III. ii. 288 et seq.

connotes indirection and a sense of 'let time take me where it will'. An ambling horse will stray off the path to munch at choice greenery; the rider does not care where he is going, or at any rate how soon he gets there. We are reminded of Tristram Shandy's method of telling his story.[33]

The thief's progress again implies a different temporal epistemology; this time it is quite easily understood. Time 'flies' for the condemned man in its conventional way.

The lawyers present interesting problems. If they 'sleep between term and term', surely for them clock time flits by instantaneously: but according to Shakespeare it 'stands still'. What Shakespeare means, perhaps, is that subjective time is composed of changes and becomingness: if there is no change or becoming, time stands still. The lawyers 'perceive not how Time moves'.

It is clear that the operative words one would use to describe time in this passage would be 'past', 'present', and 'future'. Time here *is* movement, pace, change; man's life as the journey, not the road. Equally important here is the subjectivity of the temporal viewpoint. Rosalind sees her young maid, priest, rich man, thief, and lawyers not from the point of view of an impartial objective observer, but from their own point of view. Each has his own individual way of existing, his own perception of time. Rosalind is concerned not with what they appear to be externally, but what they feel themselves to be inside. Time is not something laid out inevitably before one, but is the motion of the present moment on which one rides into the unknown and non-existent world of the future, making it first exist and then part of the past. Man's life from this viewpoint can be full of meanings and direction: the young maid and the thief on his way to the gallows both see all their lives in relation to one hoped-for or feared event, some central fact that gives everything significance.

Rosalind, as we have seen earlier, is not 'above it all'; although her philosophy is more profound, perhaps, than Jaques', she is not 'philosophical'; she herself is in a plight not much different from that of her 'young maid'.

[33] See William Holtz, 'Time's Chariot and *Tristram Shandy*', *Michigan Quarterly Review*, vol. v (Summer 1966), pp. 197–203.

Elsewhere in the play the lovers' view of time is enlarged and elucidated for us. One of the most important aspects of it is the true lover's insistence on punctuality:

Orl: My fair Rosalind, I come within an hour of my promise.
Ros: Break an hour's promise in love! He that will divide a minute into a thousand parts, and break but a part of the thousand part of a minute in the affairs of love, it may be said of him that Cupid hath clapp'd him o' th' shoulder, but I'll warrant him heart-whole.[34]

The true lover is concerned not with measurable and divisible time, but with moments. The punctuality Rosalind insists on can be explained in terms of the etymology of the word. The Latin *punctus* means 'point'; for 'punctual' Webster gives '1. of or like point'. The lovers' time is a series of points; a temporal approximation is not good enough. The present moment is not an infinitesimal portion of the minute in which we are (if it were, then Zeno's paradox would have no solution); it is like a point, it has no temporal thickness.

Modern manuals on sex have familiarized us with the virtues of timing in love-making. For Rosalind proper timing is all-important. One wonders whether there is not a pun in 'if you break one jot of your promise, *or come one minute behind your hour,* I will think you the most pathetical break-promise, and *the most hollow lover* . . . that may be chosen out of the gross band of the unfaithful'.[35] In one of the earliest slang dictionaries in the English language,[36] a 'coming-woman' is glossed as a woman who is 'free' of her 'flesh' or a 'breeding woman'. Elsewhere in Shakespeare the pun on 'come' would deepen and extend the meaning.[37] Whether or not this reading can be upheld, one of the important features of lovers' time is the idea of temporal appropriateness, of timing, of the significance of one moment as opposed to another.

[34] IV. i. 40 et seq.   [35] IV. i. 169. My italics.
[36] *A New Dictionary of the Terms Ancient and Modern of the Canting Crew* by 'B. E., Gent', 1690.
[37] e.g. *Romeo and Juliet*, II. iv. 94, *Antony and Cleopatra*, V. ii. 285, etc.

The present is what is of importance to the Shakespearean lover:

> This carol they began that hour,
> With a hey, and a ho, and a hey nonino,
> How that a life was but a flower,
> In the spring time, etc.
>
> And therefore take the present time,
> With a hey, and a ho, and a hey nonino,
> For love is crowned with the prime,
> In the spring time, etc.[38]

This is living time, the only time we exist, the present moment.

The enemy and test of lovers' time is 'historical' time. 'Well,' says Rosalind, 'Time is the old justice that examines all such offenders, and let Time try.'[39] Teasingly she assumes the attitudes of Jaques or Touchstone in order to wring denials out of Orlando: 'Say "a day" without the "ever". No, no, Orlando; men are April when they woo, December when they are wed: maids are May when they are maids, but the sky changes when they are wives.'[40] This echoes Jaques' view in its generalization and assumed 'philosophical' detachment; and Touchstone's in its subordination of love to the natural cycle. True love must ultimately deny both 'historical' and 'natural' time; though it must also find some reconciliation or *modus vivendi* with them. (The tragedy of *Romeo and Juliet* is that the reconciliation is not made with 'historical' time, the time of the Montagues and Capulets; and it is snuffed out or smothered by it. The tragedy of *Troilus and Cressida* and *Othello*, on the other hand, is that there is a compromise with 'historical' and 'natural' time, and not a true reconciliation. See Chapter 6.)

In *As You Like It* such a reconciliation can and does take place. In the 'lover and his lass' song, love is reconciled with the natural cycle:

> It was a lover and his lass,
> With a hey, and a ho, and a hey nonino,
> That o'er the green corn-field did pass

---

[38] V. iii. 24 et seq.
[39] IV. i. 177. The same idea, of time as judge, can be found in *The Winter's Tale*. See Chapter 8.   [40] IV. i. 130 et seq.

In the spring time, the only pretty ring time
When birds do sing, hey ding a ding, ding.
Sweet lovers love the spring.[41]

The great seasons allow a time for love: nature is not essentially
opposed to the spiritual movements of man. This reconciliation
is brought about thematically by the use of the idea of musical
'time': the rhythm and temporal order of a song can form a
bridge between the great natural rhythms and the smaller human
ones. The pages who sing the song indicate its significance: 'We
kept time, we lost not our time.'[42] Touchstone, who has con-
sistently reduced human significances to subhuman natural
drives, cannot accept the musical reconciliation: 'I count it but
time lost to hear such a foolish song';[43] applying the judgments
of expediency to it. 'What use is it? It is only a waste of time.' The
verdict of Jaques on Touchstone is that 'Time, the old justice
that examines all such offenders', will find him wanting: '. . . thy
loving voyage Is but for two months victuall'd.'[44] It is significant
that when Hymen characterizes the nature of Touchstone's
alliance with Audrey, she uses a seasonal image: 'as the winter
to foul weather'.[45] But Touchstone has served his purpose. He
too is a test, an assay. His function, as his name implies, is to
point out true love where it exists, to distinguish gold from base
metal.

Touchstone rejects the song; Jaques rejects the dance. At the
end of the play, we are shown another rhythmic reconciliation:

... you brides and bridegrooms all,
With measure heap'd in joy, to th' measures fall.[46]

Dancing is one of the ways we ritually reconcile the individual
with society. The measures of the dance bring together modera-
tion and joy; social, or 'historical' time is reconciled with individual or 'personal' time. Jaques cannot accept this. Though he
recognizes Orlando's 'true faith,'[47] he states that he is 'for other
than for dancing measures';[48] 'to see no pastime I'[49] he insists—a
sentiment almost identical to Touchstone's when he reacts to the
'spring time' song.

[41] v. iii. 14 et seq.   [42] v. III. 35.   [43] v. iii. 36.
[44] v. iv. 186.   [45] v. iv. 130.   [46] v. iv. 172, 173.
[47] v. iv. 182.   [48] v. iv. 187.   [49] v. iv. 189.

Obviously the most important thing about the last scene of *As You Like It* is its marriages. Helen Gardner, in a penetrating discussion of the difference between comedy and tragedy, declares: 'The great symbol of pure comedy is marriage by which the world is renewed, and its endings are always instinct with a sense of fresh beginnings. Its rhythm is the rhythm of the life of mankind, which goes on and renews itself as the life of nature does.'[50] Marriage is the reconciliation of the subjective faith, love, and hope of the individual, the objectivity and commonsense of society, and the mighty forces of fertile nature:

> You to a love that your true faith doth merit;
> You to your land, and love, and great allies;
> You to a long and well-deserved bed . . .[51]

Marriage can contain love, a legal contract, and sex in an extraordinary harmony. 'Personal', 'historical', and 'natural' time are reconciled in its sacrament, its 'blessed bond':[52]

> Then is there mirth in heaven,
> When earthly things made even
> Atone together.[53]

What Jaques and Touchstone have to say is indeed valid, within limits. If their basilisk eye of satire and cynicism were not open in all of us, we should be very impractical creatures. More important, if their viewpoints were not represented in the play we should soon lose sympathy with the highfalutin' dialectics of romantic love. Jaques and Touchstone inoculate us: and they prepare us for the grand reconciliation that is to be performed by the other great comic character in the play, Rosalind herself.

Other themes in *As You Like It* which are connected with the theme of time, such as providence, false and true sight, and outward appearance and inner reality, may be better dealt with in the next chapter on *Twelfth Night*. The marvellous modulation by which Shakespeare makes every play an individual organism, based on its own characteristic symbolic and philosophical structure, may be clearly seen in the comparison of these two 'romantic comedies'.

[50] Op. cit.   [51] v. iv. 182 et seq.   [52] v. iv. 136.
[53] v. iv. 102 et seq.

4. Season and Mask in Twelfth Night

AT first glance, many of Shakespeare's Comedies contain something, that, without going deeper, we might call escapism. In *A Midsummer Night's Dream* the young lovers escape completely from the daylight world into an enchanted forest of the night; in *As You Like It* all the main characters forsake the hard, political, and realistic world of the court for an idyllic and pastoral mode of existence. Most of the Comedies take place in an unreal world, spatially removed from the experience of the Elizabethan playgoer, where improbabilities of the plot are not only tolerable but positively delightful. '. . . Those things do best please me', says Puck, 'That befall prepost'rously';[1] where the eccentricities of the Comedies are concerned, we are inclined to agree with him.

But if Shakespeare does take his audience outside 'real life', we may be sure that he does so with designs on our apprehension and perception of it. Out in the forest Touchstone is free to flay the affectations of the Elizabethan court; in the shadows of fairyland we are shown some of the essential realities of love and imagination. Moreover Shakespeare is very conscientious about bringing his audience down to the ground again. At the end of *Love's Labour's Lost* we are given images of the groaning wretches in hospital and of the everyday country existence that lay behind the glitter of London. Shakespeare takes especial care to 'distance' us from the drama here, by an actual mention of the fact that it is all just a play:

> *Ber*: Our wooing doth not end like an old play:
>   Jack hath not Jill . . .
> *King*: Come, sir, it wants a twelvemonth an' a day,
>   And then 'twill end.
> *Ber*:   That's too long for a play.[2]

This is far from the theatrical bravado of Fabian's 'If this were

---

[1] *A Midsummer Night's Dream*, III. ii. 120 et seq.
[2] *Love's Labour's Lost*, V. ii. 862 et seq.

play'd upon a stage now, I could condemn it as an improbable
fiction'.[3] Instead of being so sure of his audience's suspension of
disbelief that he is able to make fun of it, in the passage from
Love's Labour's Lost Shakespeare is deliberately undermining
their belief and involvement in the play, making them conscious
that they are being brought back by stages to reality. The same
thing happens elsewhere in the Comedies:

> If we shadows have offended,
> Think but this, and all is mended,
> That you have but slumb'red here
> While these visions did appear.
> And this weak and idle theme,
> No more yielding but a dream,
> Gentles, do not reprehend . . .[4]

It is not the fashion to see the lady the epilogue; but it is no more
unhandsome than to see the lord the prologue. If it be true that
good wine needs no bush, 'tis true that a good play needs no
epilogue . . .[5]

This gentle weaning of the audience away from the unreal
world of the play occurs once more at the very end of Shakespeare's career, when Prospero dismisses the masque of spirits,
gives back the book and staff with which he organized the action
of the play, and finally begs pardon of the audience for breaking
the spell of the magic island and going back to his dukedom.

In *Twelfth Night*, beyond the transposition of the characters
into a fantastic location (Illyria), there is a further, temporal as
opposed to spatial, removal of the action from 'real life'. The
people in *Twelfth Night* are on holiday: there is much in the
play to suggest that this holiday corresponds with the great ritual
holiday of Winter; sharing its origins (among other things) with
the Roman *Saturnalia*, and including Christmas and Yule, which
the Elizabethans celebrated with such gusto. Obviously we would
falsify the play if we were to interpret it solely in terms of the
winter rituals; but an understanding of the mood of the Eliza-

---

[3] *Twelfth Night*, III. iv. 121 et seq.
[4] *A Midsummer Night's Dream*, V. i. 412 et seq.
[5] *As You Like It*, Epilogue. ll. 1 et seq.

bethan midwinter celebrations will illuminate many of the peculiar features of the play and deepen our appreciation of others.

C. L. Barber in his book *Shakespeare's Festive Comedy* remarks that 'the seasonal feasts were not, as now, rare curiosities to be observed by folklorists in remote villages, but landmarks framing the cycle of the year, observed with varying degrees of sophistication by most elements in the society'.[6] The function of such a ritual, as with the rituals surrounding birth, puberty, marriage, and death, is to mark, celebrate, and introduce into human and social terms, a change; whether it be in the life of an individual, in the liturgy of religion, or in the behaviour of the elements as the seasons change. Behind this fairly rational process, the punctuation of time, there is, one suspects, a more atavistic human motive. There is more than a little sympathetic magic in these basic rituals. The marriage-rite does not merely mark the beginning of a marriage: it also purports to create a marriage; and many people feel that it can even help create happiness in marriage. New Year rites do not only commemorate a date of a month, but constitute an act of faith that a new summer will come; perhaps even an operation to ensure by magic that it will come.

Such rituals, then, do not only mark an objective change, but can create a psychological one. They consist substantially in a break with everyday reality, followed by a period of time which seems outside the ordinary time of human affairs, in which social institutions, those preservers of the *status quo* and of human security, are set at nought or overturned;[7] and concluded by a rite of re-integration into normal social time. Barber expresses this element of permitted chaos thus: 'The instability of an interregnum is built into the dynamics of misrule . . .'[8]

But such rituals are not merely a relaxation from the hard work and hard rules of ordinary life. In them, once the hierarchical superstructure of social power and status has been stripped away, are stated the enduring values of society, those

[6] C. L. Barber, *Shakespeare's Festive Comedy*, Princeton U.P., 1959, pp. 5–6.
[7] cf. '. . . in one self-born hour To plant and o'erwhelm custom'—and my comments on this passage of *The Winter's Tale* in Chapter 8.
[8] Op. cit., p. 24.

aspects of society which are the expression of the individual human souls of which it is composed. In the rituals of Misrule is expressed the basic equality of men, the essential fact that human society is not a structure only, but a community: that ultimately it is not law that keeps society together, but man's blessed gregariousness. In the Maying ceremonies the beauty and power of Man's natural sexuality is celebrated. At Easter and Christmas the central facts of Man's relationship with God are expressed in symbol and statement. It is a curiously human paradox that we should be most aware of the essential premises and values of ordinary life when we are most on holiday from it.

Barber shows interesting connections between the Elizabethan rituals and some of Shakespeare's Comedies. Whatever reservations one may have about the anthropological approach to literature, we can take it that Shakespeare does exploit the energies of these ritual holidays in some of his plays, such as *A Midsummer Night's Dream, Henry IV, Twelfth Night,* and *The Winter's Tale* (which Barber does not discuss). And such a view goes a long way toward explaining our initial feeling of escapism in the Comedies. For these ritual holidays were indeed an escape from 'real life'; but they also gave punctuation and purpose to the flow of time, they could create, as well as mark, a human change; and they were the chief means of establishing and expressing the basic truths of social and individual experience: what lies behind 'real life'. If these capabilities could be given to an artistic and dramatic artificial ritual, a play, they might indeed deepen and strengthen its effect. The journeys, shipwrecks, and exiles that begin some of the Comedies might act as a rite of separation from ordinary life, and the songs, epilogues and 'distancing' speeches that conclude them could correspond to the rite of re-integration into normal time.

Even if we rejected Barber's view of the direct connection between seasonal ritual and Shakespeare's Comedies, two aspects of his view would still be useful. Shakespeare's many references to such rituals in the plays can be seen as important in invoking the standpoint and emotion of a ritual holiday; and by analogy, we can say that perhaps some of Shakespeare's Comedies perform a similar operation to that of a ritual holiday, though they were not necessarily modelled on one.

Two themes of ritual holiday are of particular interest in connection with *Twelfth Night*: the theme of mask and the theme of seasonability. Barber says of these holidays: 'Mirth took form in morris-dances, sword-dances, wassailings, mock ceremonies of summer kings and queens and of lords of misrule, mummings, disguisings, masques . . .'[9] This element of mock, disguise, or mask, is central to the seasonal rituals. It is also one of the primary ingredients of drama. Ancient Greek actors literally wore masks, and the great tragedies were performed on ritual occasions. In its origins drama is said to have sprung from ritual: both express a basic human need to pretend to be what one is not, or to be delightfully or movingly deceived by the pretence of another. This can be clearly observed in the games of children, for example.

Twelfth Night is full of masks, disguises, and deceptions. If we were to classify them, we would find three main types of mask: the disguise put on by someone who wishes to deceive others (Viola and Sir Topas); the mask of which the wearer is unaware—when a person presents, without knowing it, a face to the world that is not his own face, exemplified in Orsino and Olivia,—and the ritual mask itself. But such a classification might obscure the fact that all the masks in the play act on the audience as ritual masks: and though *Twelfth Night* is a sophisticated and civilized entertainment, though its deceptions and disguises often express the kind of psychological complexity we find in a modern novel, this does not invalidate its deeper and more primitive effects. Viola's disguise and her unmasking create a profound subjective change in the other characters of the play: but all the play's disguises have this effect on the audience. The ritual mask is really a highly complex intellectual device for the organization and adjustment of perception and experience. All actors wear a kind of ritual mask: Shakespeare accentuates this aspect of the mask, however, by exaggerated double disguises which can cross the barrier of sex more than once. Outside the

[9] Op. cit., p. 5.

internal dynamics of a play there is another system which includes both players and audience. It is in this sphere that the ritual-dramatic mask has its peculiar effect. Both the audience and the players are aware of all the various disguises in the play, so that there is no question of a simple deception in this area of the dramatic experience. The importance of this sort of mask is not delusion, but contradiction and paradox. If a man wears an animal mask, then because our minds are stretched by the contradiction, we are able more fully to understand what is a man. If we know that the wearer of a mask is not what he looks like, we know better what he *is*.[10] Those heroines of the Comedies who wear men's clothes strike us with an overwhelming sense of their femininity. The various masks put on by the characters in the play (of mourner, lover, social success, or the man with greatness thrust upon him) help us to see what they truly are underneath, so that they grow from types into persons; and when their masks are finally removed, we can see them as viable (or inadequate) human beings. Incidentally, it is this capacity of Shakespeare's to give his characters more than one level (so that, for instance, under the comic type we can see the real person), that sets him apart from those dramatists, such as Jonson and Molière, who can create a grotesque character with a vast, colourful affectation or delusion, but do not often suggest the person whose motives created the affectation or who is deluding or being deluded.

The other aspect of seasonal ritual which is of interest is that of seasonability. There is a time for sowing and a time for harvest; there is equally a time for gravity and a time for rejoicing. Today we have almost lost this sense of temporal appropriateness, as we have moved away from a rural to an urban culture, and have left the seasons behind us. The few seasons of the year when seasonability is still important (Christmas and Easter are the most obvious) have become debased and imprecise parodies of the old holidays. But in Elizabethan times it really did matter to the way

[10] Masks, by disguising the normal, social *persona*, can often reveal the inner self. Masked people in balls and carnivals are free to express desires and thoughts normally kept hidden. Viola does this in II. iv. 105 et seq. We can also see it in Lawrence Durrell's treatment of the carnival in *Balthazar*, 1961, pp. 159–82.

one lived whether it was Lent, Advent, Midsummer, or Christ-mastide. And strong social sanctions backed up the accepted mode of behaviour in these seasons. It was as much a crime to be gloomy or officious at Christmas as it was to feast during Lent or giggle at a funeral: 'Behind the laughter at the butts there is always a sense of solidarity about pleasure, a communion embracing the merrymakers in the play and the audience, who have gone on holiday in going to a comedy.'[11]

Society united in an almost frightening way against those who violated the laws of the season. Three hundred years later the man who refuses to honour the customs of Christmas is stricken with the same terrible English disapproval. The Christmas Spirit, that mighty creature of custom and the community of ordinary people, scolds Scrooge into conformity with society; the Dickensian sentimentality about Christmas is not so different from the emotional energies that fuelled the Elizabethan celebrations. Outside it is bitterly cold: we live on the northern edge of the temperate climatic belt; it is almost a moral necessity for people to get together indoors and make merry. The spoil-sport poses a psychological threat to society's survival of winter.

Where Dickens, who lived in an age of decreasing respect for seasonability, was forced to place the most severe moral pressures on his nonconformist, the Elizabethans, who were secure in the almost universal acceptance of the holiday customs, were content to drive their errant sheep back to the fold by mockery, satire, and communal laughter.

In the Sonnets time is almost always an enemy. In *Twelfth Night* we are shown how time can be an ally, if it is used properly. One of the most effective ways that society has found to harmonize itself and its members with the rhythms of time is the seasonal ritual; and Shakespeare adopts here some of the mechanisms of such ritual to bring about such a relationship with time on the part of the characters and, to some extent, the audience. In doing so, he organizes our experience in a special way and states some of the basic values of human community.

In the first scene in which Sir Toby appears we are assured that

[11] C. L. Barber, op. cit., pp. 8–9.

he considers himself on holiday, even if other members of the household are not:

> Sir To: What a plague means my niece to take the death of her brother thus? I am sure care's an enemy to life.
> Mar: By my troth, Sir Toby, you must come in earlier o'nights; your cousin, my lady, takes great exceptions to your ill hours.
> Sir To: Why, let her except before excepted.
> Mar: Ay, but you must confine yourself within the modest limits of order.
> Sir To: Confine! I'll confine myself no finer than I am. These clothes are good enough to drink in . . .[12]

With Sir Toby's roar of 'Confine!' we catch an echo of Falstaff. And indeed the same confusion of moral and physical confines is made in *2 Henry IV*:

> Ch. Just: Well, the truth is, Sir John, you live in great infamy.
> Fal: He that buckles himself in my belt cannot live in less.[13]

Sir Toby refuses to abide by rules or to limit himself: he wishes to escape those necessary sacrifices that give a human being definition, direction, a moral posture, and a recognizable character. There are many things that a man can be; most of us have to choose one or a group of these; Sir Toby tries to be all of them. The moral dangers of such an attempt are set forth by Dickens in the character of Harold Skimpole in *Bleak House*. In order to live this kind of life one must let others pay one's bills: and one cannot do this indefinitely.

Such is an everyday moral picture of Sir Toby. But it is not the judgement of the holiday world: it is not the way we see him in the first three Acts of the play. For Sir Toby is appropriate to the holiday world. On holiday we confine ourselves no finer than we are. When the Elizabethans set up a Lord of Misrule they were celebrating and symbolizing such a release from ordinary boundaries; on holiday 'to go to bed after midnight is to go to bed betimes':[14] the temporal order is reversed. In 'real life' Sir Toby is a dissolute old man: but on holiday he has character. For character consists in an adjustment or harmony with one's environ-

[12] I. iii. 1 et seq.   [13] *2 Henry IV*, I. ii. 130 et seq.
[14] II. iii. 8.

ment: Falstaff is a gigantic character of mirth in the tavern, even if he is something of a criminal on an English battlefield.

Sir Toby's behaviour is seasonable: cakes and ale are appropriate to the time of winter feasting. Shakespeare explains this in terms of rhythm:

> *Mal*: . . . Is there no respect of place, persons, nor time, in you?
> *Sir To*: We did keep time, sir, in our catches.[15]

Sir Toby has caught the rhythm of the time: we may find a passage of T. S. Eliot appropriate:

> . . . Keeping time,
> Keeping the rhythm in their dancing
> As in their living in the living seasons
> The time of the seasons and the constellations
> The time of milking and the time of harvest
> The time of the coupling of man and woman
> And that of beasts. Feet rising and falling.
> Eating and drinking. Dung and death.[16]

Among other things, the Winter Holiday celebrated the importance of the natural rhythms of life, at the turning-point of the year. Dancing is an important part of such rituals, expressing as it does the rhythm within human beings and the strength of community (since dancing is one of our most communal activities):

> Why dost thou not go to church in a galliard and come home in a coranto? My very walk should be a jig; I would not so much as make water but in a sink-a-pace. . .[17]

This dancing way of life, in tune with the great seasonal rhythms and the smaller human rhythms (and even reconciling them), has a limited value: its devotees cannot reach the sublimer regions of human experience, which negate rhythm and recurrence; but it has a recognizable and important part to play in our existence. We are in danger, if, like Hamlet, we attempt to neglect our material aspect, our animality, in an obsession with our angelic one.

At the end of the play, however, when the twins are reunited, when courting turns into marriage, when the main characters

---

[15] II. iii. 88 et seq.   [16] *East Coker*, ll. 39–46.   [17] I. iii. 119 et seq.

cease playing and start living, the holiday is at an end. Like Falstaff, Sir Toby is rejected by his creator: he appears as a drunken old man with a broken head. It is sad, but it is according to the rules of the ruthless game that Sir Toby has chosen to play. There is something cruel about seasonal ritual: at its end the Lord of Misrule is toppled from his throne, and the revellers are silenced.

If Sir Toby's behaviour is seasonable in terms of the Winter Holiday, Malvolio's is quite the opposite. He lives entirely within a set of rules and is incapable of harmonizing himself with the mood of the holiday moment. If we insist that his mood sorts very well with Olivia's, it might be replied that Olivia, too, is in a disharmonious relationship with her temporal environment, and when she comes to her senses, she is as incapable of taking Malvolio seriously as the others: 'Alas, poor fool, how have they baffl'd thee'[18]—laughter is not far below the surface.

But Malvolio is not only a figure of fun. He constitutes a considerable threat to the holiday mood, like a small, selfish boy who will not join in a game and conform to its spirit and rules. He attacks the Fool:

> I marvel your ladyship takes delight in such a barren rascal; I saw him put down the other day with an ordinary fool that has no more brain than a stone. Look you now, he's out of his guard already; unless you laugh and minister occasion to him, he is gagg'd.[19]

Precisely. In order for holiday foolery to be successful, it must be accepted in its own spirit and affirmed by all the members of the community. If there is something discordant in its environment, it cannot work. A religious ceremony requires a certain decorum on the part of those who are present: so too does a fool. This invalidates neither the foolery nor the ceremony: and anyone who is as cruel or crass as Malvolio in disturbing its atmosphere deserves a fate like Malvolio's. We should not pity Malvolio, but join in the ridicule of him; for he is aiming a blow at the precious and fragile comradeship of humanity.

The Fool is closely connected with the Holiday. Whereas the Holiday is the periodical inoculation of society with what lies

[18] v. i. 356.   [19] I. v. 78 et seq.

beyond and beneath it, the Fool is the constant reminder to society of these areas of experience. Those figures who live on the edge of society are very important to it. Wordsworth, looking at the England that the Eighteenth Century had created, whose principles had been invalidated by the French Revolution, found his consolation and justification of society in those odd characters who stand at the border of the social world—half-wits, old men, and blind people, little children, wanderers, and strangers, even the leech-gatherer himself. These figures represent common humanity and act as the *fines* of society; and they point beyond society to the values and forces that society cannot comfortably contain, but without which it is lifeless. Though Feste is no numinous village idiot, he still preserves the tradition of God's holy fools, and presides over the feast of Twelfth Night with the total franchise of those weaklings of society that society must in conscience protect. When Malvolio attacks the Fool he is committing a minor crime against the basic values of society, those values which are violated in a far more terrible, but not qualitatively different, way by Macbeth. The Fool's only defence outside the world of wit and banter is his defencelessness, like that of a guest or a kinsman.

The most salient feature of Malvolio's disharmony with his temporal environment is his obsession with the future. 'To be Count Malvolio!'[20] he says to himself; Fabian comments 'look how imagination blows him':[21] imagination, that faculty which in Shakespeare deals with the future.[22] Malvolio cannot 'take the present time'[23] and adjust himself to it: he must look ahead, betraying the present to an ambitious future.[24] This is a dangerous course from a moral point of view: it involves a man in dead time, and to do this is to surrender one's freedom; one becomes a series of effects of external circumstances. There is a curious inflexibility in Malvolio: having conceived an ambitious future for himself, and having been convinced by external (impersonal) indications—such as false handwriting—that these ambitions

---

[20] II. v. 32.   [21] II. v. 40.
[22] See Chapter 7 on Macbeth and the Imagination.
[23] *As You Like It*, v. iii. 28.
[24] Again like Macbeth: see my comments in Chapter 7.

are possible, he pursues his future ends with a monomaniac and comic obsession. He becomes a puppet whom Maria can operate with a jerk of the strings. All those forces that can rob a man of his freedom—ambition, the desire for status, even lust—become his masters.

The yellow stockings and cross-garters that Malvolio feels he must wear to gain Olivia's love are an image of his reliance on externals; they restrict, as it were, the spiritual circulation. Like Leontes in *The Winter's Tale* he becomes suddenly very acute at noticing external details in other people that accord with his obsession:

> And when she went away now—'Let this fellow be look'd to'. 'Fellow' not 'Malvolio' nor after my degree, but 'fellow'.[25]

The ratiocinative faculty, when cut off from the ordinary commonsense of the human heart, can be very energetic, though it has lost contact with the sources of truth. There is even a hint of a cerebral and anticipatory sensuality here:

> Calling my officers about me, in my branch'd velvet gown. having come from a day-bed—where I have left Olivia sleeping—[26]

Malvolio, like the worldly young man of the Sonnets, the corrupt justicers in *Lear*, and the usurper in *Macbeth*, puts on clothes that do not accord with his inner self, in order to fulfil a temporal purpose. And such a masking of the self (partly a deliberate deception of others, and partly a self-deception) is often associated with false sight and corrupt perception:

> O, you are sick of self-love, Malvolio, and taste with a distemper'd appetite. To be generous, guiltless, and of free disposition, is to take those things for bird-bolts that you deem cannon bullets.[27]

Malvolio exaggerates affronts to his person, because of his sense of self-importance, which is rooted in his obsessive ambition. Because he is unable to live for the present, what he perceives in the present is falsified. True perception cannot exist when the

[25] III. iv. 71 et seq.   [26] II. v. 44 et seq.   [27] I. v. 85 et seq.

individual is out of harmony with his environment: in this case, with the temporal environment of the Winter Holiday. Feste perhaps suggests this when Malvolio is locked up as a madman:

> I say there is no darkness but ignorance; in which thou art more puzzled than the Egyptians in their fog.[28]

Malvolio is ultimately a paradox. He thinks he can see clearly, but can only see clearly what accords with his obsession; he is a 'time-pleaser'[29] in the sense that his aims are temporal and he ingratiates himself with his mistress's self-indulgent mood; but is out of tune with the times in the sense that he cannot catch the mood of the holiday moment.

Sir Toby and Malvolio constitute the extremes within whose context move the more serious characters.

Orsino has donned the mask of the conventional lover, though he does not really know he is wearing it. He has deceived himself into believing he is in love, but it is all in his mind: he does not know Olivia at all well, we never see him in her presence until the end of the play, he never acts on his love; he is not to be found pining at Olivia's gate hallooing her name to the reverberate hills. We get the impression that if Olivia appeared by his couch she would be an embarrassing interruption to his amorous frenzy. His stiff formality with her when they actually meet is deliciously comic.

But such a self-deception can be dangerous. Although Orsino's threat to 'sacrifice the lamb'[30] that he loves is absurdly theatrical, it shows that Orsino is willing to defend his delusion by an act that would be tragic.

Like Malvolio, Orsino is out of tune with the time. Holiday cannot tolerate egotistical romantic seriousness any more than it can stand officiousness or puritanism. Romantic love is in any case a kind of puritanism, for it denies value to anything that is not of its own substance. Orsino's particular disharmony with the time consists to some extent in an obsession with the future. Orsino is almost lascivious as he looks forward to that time when all Olivia's 'perfections' are 'supplied' and 'fill'd' with 'one self

[28] IV. ii. 41 et seq.   [29] II. iii. 138.   [30] V. i. 124.

king'.[31] He is unable to live in the present: he quickly tires of all entertainment, and the Fool attributes to him a mind of opal. That love which devalues other things and makes the activities of the present moment nothing in themselves, only playthings of the romantic imagination, is always suspect in Shakespeare. We can contrast Orsino's mood with that of Sebastian, who, after his lightning courtship with Olivia, stands reeling in the garden and sees the world as if for the first time:

> This is the air; that is the glorious sun;
> This pearl she gave me, I do feel't and see't;
> And though 'tis wonder that enwraps me thus,
> Yet 'tis not madness.[32]

It is this sense of wonder that is perhaps the hallmark of true love in Shakespeare: the heightening and sharpening of the powers of the senses. Orsino does not feel wonder but boredom; his senses are not clear but congested and somewhat corrupt:

> If music be the food of love, play on,
> Give me excess of it, that, surfeiting,
> The appetite may sicken and so die.
> That strain again! It had a dying fall;
> O, it came o'er my ear like the sweet sound
> That breathes upon a bank of violets,
> Stealing and giving odour! Enough, no more;
> 'Tis not so sweet now as it was before.[33]

The synaesthesia produces a confused and almost sickly effect: all love that has an element of self-indulgence in it must pervert the senses to some extent. When what is being perceived is different in kind from what is in the mind, when Orsino, for instance, is lying listening to music but with his mind on Olivia's charms, such a perversion is likely. It is a common feature of sex-fantasies and daydreams. The mind is cut off from reality, and the senses, ordinarily the means of contact between them, are confused and chaotic. Shakespeare heightens this sickly atmosphere by contrasting it with that of the bleak sea-coast of the next scene, with its stark realities of life and death.

[31] I. i. 38, 39.   [32] IV. iii. 1 et seq.   [33] I. i. 1 et seq.

Olivia, too, wears a mask—the mask of the mourner. To 'season'[34] a brother's dead love with tears is unseasonable: death should be mourned, as ritual demands, and having been mourned, it should be forgotten; certainly it should not be allowed to interfere with the living of one's life in the present. Olivia is living in the past; this again is something one must not do on a holiday. Sir Toby is sure that 'care's an enemy to life';[35] and in this case he is right. The Fool illustrates the folly of her mourning:

> *Clo*: Good madonna, why mourn'st thou?
> *Oli*: Good fool, for my brother's death.
> *Clo*: I think his soul is in hell, madonna.
> *Oli*: I know his soul is in heaven, fool.
> *Clo*: The more fool, madonna, to mourn for your brother's soul being in heaven. Take away the fool, gentlemen.[36]

We feel that Olivia's mourning is something of a luxury, like Orsino's love: as with all those who live in the past, her mourning gives her a fixed purpose in life, that can alleviate the problems of living in the present and making such changes and decisions of the heart as are necessary in the present. We do not believe that Olivia is really still suffering from her brother's death: but she thinks she is, and this gives her a comfortable and convenient posture in life that does not require moral effort. The contrast with Viola, who has just lost a brother herself, is instructive. Viola exorcises the pain with a gift, collects to herself what hope there is in the situation, and practically settles down to creating a place in the society in which she finds herself:

> For saying so, there's gold.
> Mine own escape unfoldeth to my hope,
> Whereto thy speech serves for authority,
> The like of him. Know'st thou this country? etc.[37]

Viola's desire to fit into the life of Illyria contrasts with the anti-social behaviour of Olivia (who has 'abjur'd the company And sight of men')[38] and of the Duke who is, he says, 'best When least in company'.[39]

[34] I. i. 30.   [35] I. iii. 2.   [36] I. v. 61 et seq.   [37] I. ii. 18 et seq.
[38] I. ii. 40, 41.   [39] I. iv. 36, 37.

Olivia, like Malvolio and Orsino, finds her senses deceptive and misleading, and like Shakespeare himself in Sonnet 114 she fears 'to find Mine eye too great a flatterer to my mind'; her false sight is demonstrated by the fact that she falls in love with a woman:

> Fortune forbid my outside have not charm'd her!
> She made good view of me; indeed, so much
> That methought her eyes had lost her tongue . . .
> I am the man. If it be so—as 'tis—
> Poor lady, she were better love a dream.
> Disguise, I see thou art a wickedness
> Wherein the pregnant enemy does much.
> How easy is it for the proper-false
> In women's waxen hearts to set their forms! [40]

Olivia mourned a memory, and now loves a dream. The themes of mask and of false sight come together in this passage, which is full of the ironies of self-deception. If mourning, for Olivia, is just a mask, then she will be the more easily taken in by a mask.

Without Viola *Twelfth Night* might almost have been one of those brilliant, heartless comedies in which the author creates and flays a cast of affected or hypocritical cyphers (*Volpone* is a good example of this). Of course it is wrong to speculate in this way, if we are to be critically rigorous: a play is the total of all its words, gestures, and characters and to remove one element of it is to discuss a phantom. But such a way of looking at the play isolates all the warmth and depth of emotion which Viola brings to it.

Like most of the other main characters Viola wears a mask. But she is, unlike the others, aware that she is wearing it; and forced to present a face to the world that is not her own. Viola's mask is not the luxury of the bored, well-fed aristocrat or the expedient lie of the social climber. Her mask is a necessary limitation of her personality, and protective colouring in a world that makes deception necessary for her survival. Instead of a self-indulgent experiment in personality, a luxuriating of the self, her mask is a burden and a prison to her. Olivia and the Duke are

[40] II. ii. 16 et seq.

trying out what it feels like to be a mourner or a lover, and con-
vincing themselves that they really are. Not content with the
ordinary limitations of themselves, they overflow into shapes that
are alien to their true personalities. But Viola accepts her disguise as a disguise, and even manages to express her own personality through it: though she cannot show her sexual love for
Orsino, yet she can express a delicate and pure affection for him,
and can build up a kind of elder brother–younger brother relationship with him. This friendship between Viola and Orsino is
one of the most beautiful things in the play: Shakespeare feels
that this sort of friendship is at the heart of a true sexual relationship, though it is normally obscured by the more obvious and
physical emotions between a man and a woman. Shakespeare
and Viola explore by means of her disguise the spiritual centre
of sexual love, of which sex is only the expression. Those
conversations between Viola and the Duke are exquisite in their
warmth and gentle irony:

> *Duke*: ... How dost thou like this tune?
> *Vio*: It gives a very echo to the seat
>   Where Love is thron'd.
> *Duke*:   Thou dost speak masterly.
>   My life upon't, young though thou art, thine eye
>   Hath stay'd upon some favour that it loves;
>   Hath it not, boy?
> *Vio*:   A little, by your favour.
> *Duke*: What kind of woman is't?
> *Vio*:   Of your complexion.
> *Duke*: She is not worth thee, then. What years, i' faith?
> *Vio*: About your years, my lord.
> *Duke*: Too old, by heaven! Let still the woman take
>   An elder than herself; so wears she to him,
>   So sways she level in her husband's heart.
>   For, boy, however we do praise ourselves,
>   Our fancies are more giddy and unfirm,
>   More longing, wavering, sooner lost and won,
>   Than women's are.
> *Vio*:   I think it well, my lord.
> *Duke*: Then let thy love be younger than thyself,

Or thy affection cannot hold the bent;
For women are as roses, whose fair flow'r
Being once display'd doth fall that very hour.
Vio: And so they are; alas, that they are so!
To die, even when they to perfection grow![41]

I have quoted this dialogue at length because it illustrates many of the most charming elements in the play. We note the gentle yet authoritative tone of the Duke—his humility and wisdom here contrast with his self-dramatization a few lines later when he is thinking about Olivia. When he is in conversation with Viola he describes men's fancies as 'more giddy and unfirm . . . than women's are'; but later he asserts that women's hearts 'lack retention'; 'make no compare', he says, between the love of a woman and 'that I owe Olivia'.[42] We can admire the depth and complexity which Shakespeare creates in his characters: beneath the mask of the lover with its absurd rhetoric there is a person for whom we can feel affection and interest. And it is Viola who brings this out in him: in the context of his friendship with her he becomes what he really is, and the mask is stripped away.

Viola has a similar effect on Olivia. Swiftly she breaks through Olivia's coldness and reserve: soon the conventional mourner is gone and we see the woman beneath. Olivia makes some attempt to defend herself against the invasion of her personality by this extraordinarily dynamic force that has come into her life. First she pretends not to be the lady of the house; this pretence gone, she stands on her dignity; next, Viola persuades her to remove her mourner's veil; her final defence is wit, but at last even this barrier to the revelation of her self is down, and she swears:

Cesario, by the roses of the spring,
By maidhood, honour, truth, and every thing,
I love thee so that, maugre all thy pride,
Nor wit nor reason can my passion hide.[43]

Viola's disguise, by its rudeness, wit, and warmth has cracked Olivia's shell: even if Olivia loves a 'dream' she has at least started existing in and making some response to the real world.

[41] II. iv. 19 et seq.   [42] II. iv. 100 et seq.   [43] III. i. 146 et seq.

She has become involved at last, and if her involvement is with a disguise, this is only justice, a punishment for her own self-disguise. Olivia realizes that she has been misusing her time, that the present moment is something valuable, and to mourn the past is a sin: 'The clock upbraids me with the waste of time.'[44] She has caught something of Viola's sense of urgency, the same feeling of the preciousness of life that makes Shakespeare urge his friend to have children in the Sonnets. Viola had told her:

> Lady, you are the cruell'st she alive
> If you will lead these graces to the grave
> And leave the world no copy.[45]

And Olivia responded with a gift and with the resolve that 'ourselves we do not owe'.[46] To be able to live in the present and to be able to give of oneself come down eventually to the same thing. Viola seems to have a capacity for making the Duke and Olivia come alive, so that they respond not to the past or future but to the present: so that their masks of past and future are stripped away.

The conversation which I quoted between Viola and the Duke exhibits not only the beauty of their relationship beneath their masks, but also an underlying note of sadness in the play. Women are as roses, says the Duke: and Viola agrees with what sounds like a sigh. Feste sings:

> What is love? 'Tis not hereafter;
> Present mirth hath present laughter;
> What's to come is still unsure
> In delay there lies no plenty
> Then come kiss me, sweet and twenty;
> Youth's a stuff will not endure.[47]

This is reminiscent of the spring song in *As You Like It*:

> This carol they began that hour,
> With a hey, and a ho, and hey nonino,
> How that a life was but a flower,
> In the spring time, etc.

[44] III. i. 127.
[45] I. v. 225. Olivia's bantering attempt to itemize her beauty and thus preserve it, only demonstrates the impossibility of making a valid record of beauty. Shakespeare had claimed in the Sonnets to eternalize his friend's beauty: Olivia's literalistic version of this approach shows its basic absurdity.
[46] I. v. 294.   [47] II. iii. 46 et seq.

> And therefore take the present time,
> With a hey, and a ho, and a hey nonino,
> For love is crowned with the prime,
> In the spring time, etc.[48]

Behind the celebration of the values of life that took place in the holiday rituals was a deep awareness of death and of the transience of living things; demanding a realization of the poignant importance of the present moment.

In *Twelfth Night* (and indeed in *As You Like It*) time is not seen just as an enemy, but as a rhythm that can give us what we want if we set ourselves at harmony with it: a view that resembles some aspects of Stoicism. A few passages from Marcus Aurelius may be of interest here:

Therefore, make your passage through the span of time in obedience to Nature and gladly lay down your life, as an olive, when ripe, might fall, blessing her who bare it and grateful to the tree which gave it life.[49]

... each of us lives only in the present, this brief moment; the rest is either a life that is past, or is in an uncertain future.[50]

Love only what falls to your lot and is destined for you; what is more suited to you than that?[51]

... true ... judgement says to what befalls it: 'This is what you are in reality, even if you seem other in appearance.'[52]

Perfection of character possesses this: to live each day as if the last, to be neither feverish nor apathetic, and not to act a part.[53]

The healthy eye should be able to look at every object of sight, and not to say: 'I wish it were green', for this is what a man says who has ophthalmia. The healthy ear and nose must be ready for every object of hearing or smell ...[54]

It is in your power to secure at once all the objects which you dream of reaching by a roundabout path, if you will be fair to yourself: that is, if you will leave all the past behind, commit the future to Providence, and direct the present, and that alone, to Holiness and Justice ...[55]

[48] *As You Like It*, v. iii. 24 et seq.
[49] A. S. L. Farquharson, ed. and trans., *The Meditations of Marcus Aurelius Antoninus*, 1944, p. 71.   [50] Ibid., p. 45.   [51] Ibid., p. 139.
[52] Ibid., p. 145.   [53] Ibid., p. 145.   [54] Ibid., p. 211.
[55] Ibid., p. 235.

The stoic answer to the problem of transience was a refined and Confucian acceptance; resigned and somewhat world-weary, the ideal stoic involved himself in the present moment as a refuge from the storms of time. Shakespeare fills this acceptance with joy and shows the present moment not as a refuge but as the centre of life. Not that his comic world-view did not have its darker side: but even here he deepens the stoic sentiment, replacing the Roman *Weltschmerz* with more full-blooded Renaissance sorrows.

The hint of sadness in Viola gives the conception of her character extraordinary depth and beauty. The pathos, irony, and sweetness of her reply to Orsino's brag of his love for Olivia is characteristic:

> *Duke*: And what's her history?
> *Vio*: A blank, my lord. She never told her love,
>   But let concealment, like a worm i' th' bud,
>   Feed on her damask cheek. She pin'd in thought;
>   And with a green and yellow melancholy
>   She sat like Patience on a monument,
>   Smiling at grief. Was not this love indeed?[56]

Viola's description of herself is a description of the true sorrows of love, as opposed to the pettish, self-indulgent sentiment of Orsino. For even those who stand in a proper relationship with time, and who do not deceive themselves by an obsession with past or future, must suffer and pine in this way. If time is a rhythm which gives us what we want only at the appointed moment, if opportunity only comes when the time is ripe, there must be waiting, frustration, the balking of desire. The pure in heart, who are able to grasp their opportunity, are not immune to pain: for sometimes opportunity never comes. Viola does as much as she can within the limits that her situation imposes on her. But she can do no more:

> O Time, thou must untangle this, not I;
> It is too hard a knot for me t' untie![57]

But Viola's resignation to the force of time gives her, paradoxically, great powers of action: by accepting her limitations

[56] II. iv. 108 et seq.   [57] II. ii. 38, 39.

she becomes the most potent force for change in the play. Hamlet's inactivity was largely the result of a failure to let time untangle the knot of his problem: when he resigns himself to the element in which he lives, he is able to act.

Viola, then, is a paradox: resigned yet active; sad but merry; disguised but sincere. Though she is the only character who is forced to wear a mask, she is also the great unmasker. Since she is disguised, she is able to say things which reveal her own inner self and demolish the affectations and self-delusions of others: since her own *persona* is concealed, she can strip away the *personæ* of others. The ritual mask clarifies perception by paradox and contradiction, so that the truth may be seen. Because of Viola we are persuaded to look deeper into the other characters; if she is disguised, we feel, are not the others also?—

> *Vio*: ... you do think you are not what you are.
> *Oli*: If I think so, I think the same of you.
> *Vio*: Then think you right; I am not what I am.[58]

These simple sentences, with their common words and plain grammar, and their depth of complex irony and moral insight, pose basic questions about the nature of human communication:[59] what is the relationship between what I think of you, what you think of yourself, what you think of me, and my own self-image? Or, to put the problem a different way, where is the self, that entity that exists only in the infinitesimal present but which possesses a kind of timelessness? and how can it be distinguished from the temporal and deterministic accretions that surround it and by which it is expressed?

The mask or disguise of comedy is the symbol by which these problems are clarified, and time is the process by which personality is unmasked. There is in Shakespeare sometimes a certain mystical quality in the operation of time. The resurrection of Sebastian, which precipitates the unmasking of Viola and her release from her disguise, is a foretaste of the return and rescue from the sea of Thaissa, Marina, Perdita, and Ferdinand, all of

---

[58] III. i. 136.
[59] R. D. Laing's book *The Politics of Experience*, 1967, discusses them with great sensitivity.

which are closely associated with mysterious effects of time.[60] The return from the sea symbolizes for Shakespeare something in time that we could provisionally label 'providence'. Providence brings about Sebastian's reappearance, which in turn untangles the knot of Viola's predicament and releases her from her disguise. Her unmasking then produces the 'ritual mask' effect on Olivia and Orsino, as they realize their own folly and the implications of the innocent remarks Viola made under cover of her disguise. As perception is clarified, the deceptions drop away and the true selves of the characters are seen.

For those who are innocent in their dealings with time, like Viola, it will work miracles and restore a dead brother; the long waiting for an opportunity that apparently can never come is rewarded in a way which seems outside the ordinary temporal dispensation. Leontes in *The Winter's Tale* has to wait sixteen years: but an even more miraculous and unlooked-for resurrection was his reward. Olivia loses her brother, whom she had made the basis of a temporal dishonesty; Viola regains hers. Time's untangling does not stop here. Neither Olivia nor Orsino gets the spouse he or she wanted, because they wanted them in the wrong way; but they both obtain poetic justice in the form of a partner appropriate to their vices and virtues. Orsino's only honest and *present* relationship, though it was with someone he thought a man, is crowned with marriage. Olivia falls in love with an outward appearance, but marries someone else, as is only fair; but she is rewarded for her openness and self-revelation in III i. by a husband whose outward appearance is the same as that with which she fell in love. Those whose desires are rooted in a dead past or a non-existent future are fooled by time and their expectations are Puckishly contradicted. At the end of the game, Viola, whose hopes are in tune with the times, and who lives in the present, gains all she played for.

The ritual clarification has taken place, and time has been shown as ordered and backed by providence. It remains only

[60] The more complex implications of Hamlet's return from his sea voyage will be discussed later. In Chapter 8 I will analyse closely the function of time in *The Winter's Tale*, and refers to *Pericles* and the 'sea change' in *The Tempest*.

for the dramatist to bring the audience back to reality from the
world of mask and seasonable merrymaking:

> When that I was and a little tiny boy,
> With hey, ho, the wind and the rain
> A foolish thing was but a toy,
> For the rain it raineth every day.

. . . . .

> A great while ago the world began,
> With hey, ho, the wind and the rain,
> But that's all one, our play is done,
> And we'll strive to please you every day.[61]

[Note: Since writing this book I have read two essays concern-
ing the symbolic representation of time, 'Cronus and Chronos',
and 'Time and False Noses', in Edmund Leach's book *Rethinking
Anthropology*, 1961, pp. 124–36. These fascinating essays state
in an anthropological context much of what I have said in my
chapters on *As You Like It* and *Twelfth Night*, and may suggest
to the reader further elaborations of my approach in these pages.]

[61] v. ii. 375 et seq.

5. The Delay of Hamlet

THE questions that arise in *Hamlet* are not about what a man should do in a given situation with given moral principles; rather they are about the spiritual basis of morality, and about a man's psychological capability of moral action. Hamlet's problem is not moral uncertainty but spiritual darkness: not a difficulty in choosing between temporal actions in the temporal world, but in acting at all when the values and ideals he requires for action have been undermined by an evil crime; and in adjusting himself to the timeless world of the Ghost whence comes his only moral commandment, of revenge. The doubts that we, the audience, as well as Hamlet himself, may entertain as to the nature and veracity of the Ghost, and the squeamishness about revenge which is present in the play, together with the psychological and social problems that face the hero, are only peripheral to the great questions which are asked in the soliloquies—the concrete materials that Hamlet draws into his spiritual struggle, and with which the dramatist 'bodies forth' this struggle. Hamlet's spiritual disorganization is not the *result* of uncertainty about the right course of action; rather it is its *cause.*

Hamlet must act in relation to two worlds: the world of time in which the crime was committed and within which he must work his revenge; and the timeless world where he has been shown the crime and commanded to revenge it. He describes the temporal world thus:

Ham: Denmark's a prison.
Ros: Then is the world one.
Ham: A goodly one; in which there are many confines, wards, and dungeons, Denmark being one o' th' worst.[1]

Later Hamlet describes himself as 'lapsed', that is, taken prisoner, 'in time and passion'.[2] It is fairly clear in the context what he means by 'taken prisoner in passion'; what does he mean by

---

[1] II. ii. 242 et seq.   [2] III. iv. 107.

'taken prisoner in time' but that time is for him a prison, the prison of the world to which he had earlier referred?

Politically the temporal world of *Hamlet* is a world of expediency where the only criteria of action are those of policy and the main chance. Claudius is the successful Machiavellian prince, who possesses an easy mastery of any situation, the born politician's accurate, pragmatic, but superficial grasp of human motives. There is a world of political skill in Claudius' first words to his assembled court. He 'explains' how he 'personally' feels about the situation, giving his hearers the privilege, as it were, of watching the royal mind as it weighs up grave problems of state. His rhetoric appears easy and eloquent, but is in reality controlled and organized to give dignity to a single brutal fact. The decision itself—'taken to wife'—succeeds a series of parentheses as if after much heart-searching and wise hesitation: there are three lines between subject and verb, and two between object and subject. He ends this sub-section of his speech with a marvellous condescension to his advisers, giving them the illusion of power without its substance:

> ... nor have we herein barr'd
> Your better wisdoms, which have freely gone
> With this affair along. For all, our thanks.[3]

Claudius covers himself with the panoply, ritual, and decorum of kingship; but it is all false. With the tacit consent of the court, an institution, which has become internally diseased, is being preserved for the sake of security and social continuity. Surrounding the usurper are sycophants like Osric, a lesser being of the same world:

> Thus has he, and many more of the same bevy, that I know the drossy age dotes on, only got the tune of the time and outward habit of encounter—a kind of yesty collection, which carries them through the most fann'd and winnowed opinions; and do but blow them to their trial, the bubbles are out.[4]

Like the courtly flatterers whom Shakespeare so despises in the Sonnets, Osric's skill in temporal affairs covers a total emptiness of moral being. When the bubble bursts there will be nothing

---

[3] I. ii. 14 et seq.   [4] V. ii. 183 et seq.

left. Those who choose to please the time will be deserted by time's favour when their time runs out. Claudius, who does not only flatter, but also attempts to control, the deterministic forces of political cause and effect, is actually destroyed by his own plots. Rosencrantz and Guildenstern are similarly 'hoist' by their own 'petar'.[5]

Horatio is almost alone in his rejection of the temporal expedients of flattery and political manipulation:

> ... Why should the poor be flatter'd?
> No, let the candied tongue lick absurd pomp,
> And crook the pregnant hinges of the knee
> Where thrift may follow fawning ...
> ... thou hast been
> As one, in suff'ring all, that suffers nothing;
> A man that Fortune's buffets and rewards
> Hast ta'en with equal thanks ...[6]

His stoical morality insulates him from the petulance of Fortune.

Love itself is treated by the inhabitants of this world as if it were only an external show to obtain the satisfaction of temporary desires:

> For Hamlet, and the trifling of his favour,
> Hold it a fashion and a toy in blood,
> A violet in the youth of primy nature,
> Forward not permanent, sweet not lasting,
> The perfume and the suppliance of a minute ...[7]

> Virtue itself scapes not calumnious strokes;
> The canker galls the infants of the spring
> Too oft before their buttons be disclos'd;
> And in the morn and liquid dew of youth
> Contagious blastments are most imminent.[8]

There is a hint here of the inner corruption that may lurk below the outward show of love and beauty, which we have found also in the Sonnets.

In the first Act Polonius exhibits more subtly the moral confines of Denmark. He presents to us the little stock of maxims by

[5] III. iv. 207.   [6] III. ii. 57 et seq.   [7] I. iii. 5 et seq.
[8] I. ii. 38 et seq.

which all his experience is evaluated. Many of us have laughed
at the foolish counsellor; but perhaps we would not laugh if we
realized how many people have similarly given up the struggle
of growth and the evaluation of experience, and live entirely by
a little bag of precepts such as these:

> ... Give thy thoughts no tongue,
> Nor any unproportion'd thought his act.
> Be thou familiar, but by no means vulgar ... etc.[9]

Not that such commonplaces are wrong or evil; they simply possess no positive content. There is no inner spiritual life of which
these precepts are an outward manifestation. Like Claudius,
Polonius expects all men to behave as deterministically as he
does; as if all men were confined by a dead system of compulsions,
similar to his own dead system of maxims. He has substituted the
complexity of 'assays of bias' and 'indirections'[10] for the un-
expectedness of reality: and when he applies his system to
Hamlet, the results are disastrous for himself and all his family.

Polonius is strongly reminiscent of T. S. Eliot's old men who
have ceased to function spiritually and have become petrified
within a code or system; whose knowledge 'imposes a pattern,
and falsifies';[11] and whose serenity is only a 'deliberate hebe-
tude'.[12] Eliot promises them that in the last trial of death they
will be found wanting and will be 'whirled Beyond the circuit
of the shuddering Bear';[13] they 'all go into the dark'.[14] Such men
have allowed themselves to become totally limited to the objective world; and the irony of objective death will fall upon them:

> ... Indeed, this counsellor
> Is now most still, most secret, and most grave
> Who was in life a foolish prating knave.[15]

The world of Time is the world of cause and effect. The
court of Claudius moves in a narrow, deterministic system of
stimulant, motive, and formula. It is indeed the ordinariness, the
predictability, of this way of looking at the world, which we fall
back on when faced by the terrifying and the unknown. Claudius

[9] I. iii. 59 et seq.   [10] II. i. 65, 66.   [11] 'East Coker', l. 84.
[12] 'East Coker', l. 78.   [13] 'Gerontion', l. 68.   [14] 'East Coker', l. 101.
[15] III. iv. 213 et seq.

invokes this sort of 'commonsense' when he tries to coax Hamlet, the nonconformist who doesn't accept the system, into forgetfulness of his father's death:

> But you must know your father lost a father;
> That father lost, lost his . . .
> . . . But to persever
> In obstinate condolement is a course
> Of impious stubbornness; 'tis unmanly grief;
> It shows a will most incorrect to heaven . . .
> An understanding simple and unschool'd;
> For what we know must be, and is as common
> As any the most vulgar thing to sense,
> Why should we in our peevish opposition
> Take it to heart? Fie! 'tis a fault to heaven
> A fault against the dead, a fault to nature,
> To reason most absurd; whose common theme
> Is death of fathers, and who still hath cried,
> From the first corse till he that died to-day,
> 'This must be so.'[16]

—It is ironic, perhaps, that the 'first corse' was that of Abel, brother of Cain.—Claudius' words are as irrelevant to Hamlet's mental condition as if he spoke a different language; later, in conversation with Hamlet, he is to admit that 'these [i.e. Hamlet's] words are not mine'.[17] They are irrelevant because Hamlet does not accept this ordinary, commonsense, deterministic view of the world. Hamlet is not reasonable, for his deeper vision of life is not reasonable: and the Sunday-school epithets, 'obstinate', 'impious', 'unmanly', 'unschool'd', 'peevish', are not applicable to his experience. Claudius himself is to some extent a 'tedious old fool'.[18] Hamlet's judgements are not those of time and of cause and effect, but are based on spiritual and timeless values.

Judgement, then, is corrupt in the court of Claudius. But there is another side to the coin—the corruption of the blood. In this play there is no reconciliation of blood and judgement except in Horatio:

[16] I. ii. 89 et seq.   [17] III. ii. 94.   [18] II. ii. 218.

> ... and blest are those
> Whose blood and judgement are so well comeddled
> That they are not a pipe for Fortune's finger
> To sound what stop she please ...[19]

To possess a proper balance of intellectual motive and bodily impulse is indeed necessary if we are to become free of the compulsions of time. But this is not enough. We are, for instance, unhappy with the compromise solution of *Measure for Measure*, because Angelo's reformation *is* only a compromise and does not come from a positive moral source which would render the conflict between blood and judgement unnecessary. Hamlet envies Horatio his integration; but his own moral disorganization comes about not because he is morally weaker than Horatio, but because he has greater spiritual problems.[20]

In Elsinore the compulsions of the blood are neither controlled by judgement (which has become corrupt) nor assumed into a higher spiritual order. Gertrude is bound by physical craving as Polonius is bound by precept, Osric by fashion, and Claudius himself by expedience:

> ... Sense, sure, you have,
> Else could you not have motion; but sure that sense
> Is apoplex'd; for madness would not err;
> Nor sense to ecstasy was ne'er so thrall'd
> But it reserv'd some quantity of choice
> To serve in such a difference.[21]

The power of free evaluation of experience is lost in the tyranny of flesh, as Polonius had lost it in his little world of maxims. The court of Elsinore is a skin of hypocrisy stretched over a black well of corruption. As in Swift's world of the Houyhnhnms and the Yahoos, or Huxley's of the Brave New World and the Reservation, there seem to be no alternatives apart from brutal sensuality and sterile order.

Hamlet's desperate remedy for Gertrude is a compromise: to temper and control one kind of temporal tyranny he proposes another. Polonius' way of life—custom, precept and external show—is opposed to lust and craving:

[19] III. ii. 66 et seq.   [20] But see D. G. James, *The Dream of Learning*, 1951.
[21] III. iv. 71 et seq.

Assume a virtue, if you have it not.
That monster custom, who all sense doth eat,
Of habits devil, is angel yet in this,
That to the use of actions fair and good
He likewise gives a frock or livery
That aptly is put on. Refrain to-night;
And that shall lend a kind of easiness
To the next abstinence . . .[22]

Here it is Hamlet who sounds like the Sunday-school teacher: at
this stage Hamlet's own inner moral being is in a shattered and
inadequate state, and he has no positive spiritual ideal to set
against his mother's lack of ideals.

But it is not only the individual who is enslaved by the tyranny
of the flesh. Hamlet sees all history as a cycle of copulation,
death, and decay:

A man may fish with the worm that hath eat of a king, and eat
of the fish that hath fed of that worm.[23]

Why may not imagination trace the noble dust of Alexander
till 'a find it stopping a bung-hole?[24]

Why wouldst thou be a breeder of sinners?[25]

For if the sun breed maggots in a dead dog, being a good kissing
carrion . . .[26]

. . . let her paint an inch thick, to this favour she must come.[27]

Within the temporal world·this is the only end and the only
beginning.

Normally the world gets on well enough with the precepts of
the old in spirit, the motives of policy, and the impulses of the
flesh. But to Hamlet it is different. The prison of the world is not
unbearable to him because of its limitations, but because the freedom outside it is too terrible to consider:

'O God, I could be bounded in a nutshell and count myself a
king of infinite space, were it not that I have bad dreams.'[28]

It is in the land of dreams, the darkness of night, that Hamlet

[22] III. iv, 160 et seq.   [23] IV. iii. 27, 28.   [24] V. i. 198, 199.
[25] III. i. 121.   [26] II. ii. 180.   [27] V. i. 188.
[28] II. ii. 253 et seq.

>76ef> The breaking of human faith

discovers an evil which can transform the everyday, corrupt, but endurable world of time into a nightmare.

The most catastrophic event that can take place in a play by Shakespeare is the breaking of faith:

> It cannot fail but by
> The violation of my faith; and then
> Let nature crush the sides o' the' earth together
> And mar the seeds within.[29]

> ... and when I love thee not
> Chaos is come again.[30]

The breaking of human faith seems, in Shakespeare, to cause an imbalance or discontinuity in the temporal world which points to a disorder in the timeless world of values and of the spirit. Psychologically a terrible event or crime can rock our deepest faith in the beneficent powers of eternity, which we suppose to control our lives through Providence. Shakespeare's vision of disjointed time is an externalized view of something very real which takes place within the human psyche. It is as if the loss of human constancy were a symptom or cause of a universal destruction of constancy, of the regularity and order of time that gives us faith in the future, that it will not too greatly differ from the past. *Hamlet* is saturated with broken faith (not faith in the sense of mere belief or a knowledge of the probabilities of human motives, but the deeper faith in an individual that is akin to love)—the faith of Claudius to his brother, of Gertrude to her husband, of Rosencrantz and Guildenstern to their friend. Hamlet's faith in his mother, his stepfather, and his mistress is destroyed as a result. To break faith 'to' destroys faith 'in'.

Personal constancy is perhaps our only defence against time. Shakespeare says as much in Sonnet 116. In a world governed completely by the laws of time, where all things are subject to alteration, the only thing that gives us a continuing identity is faith: in a sense, what we most deeply believe in is what we are. But in this play faith has become time's slave. The Player King sounds this note:

[29] *The Winter's Tale*, IV. iv. 468 et seq. [30] *Othello*, III. iii. 92, 93.

> Purpose is but the slave to memory,
> Of violent birth, but poor validity;
> Which now, the fruit unripe, sticks on the tree;
> But fall unshaken when they mellow be.
> Most necessary 'tis that we forget
> To pay ourselves what to ourselves is debt . . .

—The loss of faith is a self-betrayal.—

> This world is not for aye; nor 'tis not strange
> That even our loves should with our fortunes change;
> For 'tis a question left us yet to prove,
> Whether love lead fortune or else fortune love.[31]

Claudius says the same thing to Laertes:

> But that I know love is begun by time;
> And that I see, in passages of proof,
> Time qualifies the spark and fire of it.
> There lives within the very flame of love
> A kind of wick or snuff that will abate it;
> And nothing is at a like goodness still . . .[32]

It is precisely this attitude that Hamlet sees in his mother at the beginning of the play. He is appalled at her swift remarriage:

> But two months dead! Nay, not so much, not two . . .
> O God! a beast that wants discourse of reason
> Would have mourn'd longer . . .
> . . . O, most wicked speed, to post
> With such dexterity to incestuous sheets![33]

His mother's matter-of-factness, her objectivity, is what astonishes him. She seems to lack completely the subjective sense of time that makes us human. He cannot see into her. She is behaving like an automaton, an animal. If faith makes us what we are, then what is Gertrude? To Hamlet she appears to have lost her personality. There is nothing fixed in the world when his mother can seem to dissolve thus before his eyes. The world is like an unweeded garden, subject to meaningless transformations; and if his flesh comes from his mother, why does it not

---

[31] III. ii. 183 et seq.   [32] IV. vii. 111 et seq.
[33] I. ii. 138 et seq.

melt and dissolve? Later his incredulity is transformed into a biting and surrealistic sarcasm:

> *Ham*: . . . look you, how cheerfully my mother looks, and my father died within's two hours.
> *Oph*: Nay, 'tis twice two months, my lord.
> *Ham*: So long? Nay then, let the devil wear black, for I'll have a suit of sables. O heavens! die two months ago, and not forgotten yet? Then there's hope a great man's memory may outlive his life half a year; but, by'r lady, 'a must build churches, then; or else shall 'a suffer not thinking on . . .[34]

Hamlet contrasts his own subjective sense of the recentness of his father's death with the objectivity of his mother. He refuses to accept the objective time that has passed since his father's death, and gets it wrong twice: he then comments that if we are completely objective, there is no reason to remember a great man unless he builds monuments that survive him.

Hamlet is also expressing the idea of untimeliness: the breaking of the natural rhythm and sequence of things. In Milton's *Lycidas* it is not death but untimeliness which is the major problem: the poet asks for an explanation from the natural deities and does not get one, for what has happened is outside the law of nature, the kingdom of the evening star, of the regular procession of the seasons. The season's flowers heaped on Lycidas' hearse are no consolation:

> . . . And with forced fingers rude
> Shatter your leaves before the mellowing year.
> Bitter constraint, and sad occasion dear,
> Compels me to disturb your season due:
> For Lycidas is dead, dead ere his prime . . .[35]

We all have a rhythm within us, which is our claim to sanity. In the meaningless and bewildering flux of time, our own little rhythms become a kind of stability. When the rhythm is disturbed, odd things can happen to us. The sense of unreality we have after missing a night's sleep or travelling by aeroplane

---

[34] III. ii. 121 et seq.   [35] *Lycidas*, ll. 4 et seq.

across several time-zones is an image of that greater sense of lost identity, verging on schizophrenia, that can affect those who have been bereaved or who have suffered a similarly catastrophic change in their ordinary routine. Ophelia reacts in this way, to the extent of complete withdrawal from reality. Hamlet fights desperately against the same sense of the basis of existence having disappeared, by stepping back from himself and allowing part of himself to go insane while preserving some core of himself intact.

This untimeliness is not merely a disruption of the natural rhythm of life. It is also a moral untimeliness. Hamlet's father did not just die before his natural end: he was murdered in the midst of all his sins. Gertrude's second marriage was not just premature: it was also incestuous. Hamlet comments:

> The time is out of joint. O cursed spite,
> That ever I was born to set it right![36]

The disjointing or interruption of the ordinary flow of time takes place with the appearance of the Ghost. The 'bringing home Of bell and burial',[37] the rituals that we use to protect ourselves against the fire and ice of eternity are to be broken asunder:

> ... tell
> Why thy canoniz'd bones, hearsed in death,
> Have burst their cerements; why the sepulchre
> Wherein we saw thee quietly enurn'd,
> Hath op'd his ponderous and marble jaws
> To cast thee up again.[38]

The events that are to follow will be outside our ordinary knowledge of death, and beyond our normal means of coping with it.

The ghost scene takes place in that period of night that Hamlet calls the 'very witching time of night':[39] the 'dead vast and middle of the night'.[40]

[36] I. v. 189.
[38] I. iv. 46 et seq.
[37] V. i. 227, 228.
[39] III. ii. 378.
[40] I. ii. 198. Alexander gives 'waste' but I prefer 'vast' for which there is as much evidence.

The earlier scene in which the watchmen discuss the Ghost contains much that should affect our attitude to these unearthly
hours between midnight and morning:

> *Mar*: It faded on the crowing of the cock.
> Some say that ever 'gainst that season comes
> Wherein our Saviour's birth is celebrated,
> This bird of dawning singeth all night long;
> And then, they say, no spirit dare stir abroad,
> The nights are wholesome, then no planets strike,
> No fairy takes, nor witch hath power to charm,
> So hallowed and so gracious is that time.
> *Hor*: So have I heard, and do in part believe it.
> But look, the morn, in russet mantle clad,
> Walks o'er the dew of yon high eastward hill . . .[41]

The cock, always the giver of time and measure, marker of the
regularity of day and night, has power to banish the Ghost. For
the Ghost inhabits the timeless period of night, where, in its
'dead vast' there is no order or measure, where there are no hard
outlines or regular changes, and time itself seems to have no
reality. As soon as the dawn and the normal diurnal cycle reassert
themselves, the Ghost fades.

The reference to the birth of Christ has alarming implications:
the appearance of the Ghost is in some sense an antithesis of the
Nativity. The Ghost is an incarnation of darkness rather than of
light. He is resurrected from the tomb, like Christ, but he brings
not the good news of the Gospel but a tale of an ultimate crime.
To Hamlet this is an evil miracle. Not that the Ghost himself is
evil; he is, if anything, a sad and noble figure, 'majestical'.[42] It is
his story and his command that are unbearable to Hamlet.

The Ghost is both outside time and also the disrupter of it.
Around him are clustered the associations of his own life as king
and soldier many years ago:

> Such was the very armour he had on
> When he the ambitious Norway combated;
> So frown'd he once when, in an angry parle,
> He smote the sledded Polacks on the ice.[43]

---

[41] I. i. 157 et seq.   [42] I. i. 143.   [43] I. i. 60 et seq.

The distinction between 'then' and 'now' disappears in a weird way; to us, who are accustomed to the recordings of the past on tape, film, or old newsreels, the effect is not so strong as it would have been to the Elizabethans.

Horatio realizes that the watchers on the wall are now on the windy edge of ordinary time. It is not safe for men to look beyond, he feels: human kind cannot bear very much reality :

> What if it tempt you toward the flood, my lord,
> Or to the dreadful summit of the cliff
> That beetles o'er his base into the sea,
> And there assume some other, horrible, form,
> Which might deprive your sovereignty of reason
> And draw you into madness? Think of it:
> The very place puts toys of desperation,
> Without more motive, into every brain
> That looks so many fathoms to the sea
> And hears it roar beneath.[44]

Shakespeare is referring to those deepest and most disquieting areas of the human psyche and its experience that poets have so often symbolized by the sea and the cliff.[45] To adventure in this area is indeed to court the dangers of monsters and madness.[46] Hamlet is daring to look beyond ordinary reality; whether we call what he sees the depth-subconscious or Nirvana does not matter. There was, according to the medieval cosmology, a sphere of sea surrounding the universe; today the biologists tell us that when our ancestors, the amphibians, crawled out of the sea, they brought with them and transmitted to us an oceanic internal environment of blood and lymph, though they had left their external environment of brine behind them. In any case, whether this eternal ocean is an internal psychological phenomenon or an external region beyond the temporal universe, Hamlet stands at its brink when he addresses the unhappy spirit, once the well-spring of his own being.

[44] I. iv. 69 et seq. The commas I have inserted before and after 'horrible' are essential to the sense.

[45] e.g. in *The Seafarer*, *The Ancient Mariner*, and 'The Dry Salvages'; also Gerald Manley Hopkins, 'No Worse, There is None', 1. 9.

[46] As in 'East Coker' 1. 92: '... menaced by monsters ...' etc.

Hamlet goes forward into the timeless world. Shakespeare suggests, rather than attempts to portray on the stage, the terrifying nature of this world:

> I could a tale unfold whose lightest word
> Would harrow up thy soul, freeze thy young blood,
> Make thy two eyes, like stars, start from their spheres,
> Thy knotted and combined locks to part,
> And each particular hair to stand an end,
> Like quills upon the fretful porpentine.[47]

Shakespeare can only describe such a world in terms of one's emotional and physical reaction to it. By a kind of unconscious mimicry, he effectively produces the same effect in his audience, so that we need not be shown anything concrete and factual that might seem banal. Indeed, there *is* nothing concrete in this world; and the Ghost accurately reveals in this way the 'secrets' of his 'prison-house'.[48]

Why does Shakespeare use the Ghost to inform Hamlet of the facts of his father's death? Could not Hamlet have discovered the crime in some ordinary way, as being told of it by a witness? Could he not have conceived the necessity for revenge in his own mind, without being commanded to fulfil it by the Ghost? The appearance of the Ghost and his story of the crime are not just an objective event for Hamlet, but also a subjective event. Hamlet does not discover the crime in that region of consciousness in which a detective, for instance, might discover it. The crime is perceived by him in the deepest regions of his spirit, and strikes at the foundations of his being. Consequently his attitude to it is not the same as the attitude of Fortinbras or Laertes to their own fathers' deaths. Hamlet's immediate reaction to the Ghost's story is instructive:

> O all you host of heaven! O earth! What else?
> And shall I couple hell?[49]

There is a sinister ambiguity about this exclamation. Hamlet invokes the beneficent forces of heaven, but now he is not sure whether he should not also call on the malefic powers. There is a further possible ambiguity of a verbal kind: 'And shall I couple

[47] I. v. 15 et seq.   [48] I. v. 14.   [49] I. v. 92, 93.

hell?' could perhaps be taken as containing a subsidiary sense:
'Shall I mate with, or become allied to, Hell?'

Furthermore, the Ghost is necessary so that revenge may be
seen not merely as a resolution conceived by Hamlet but as a
commandment from the timeless realm. The sting of the play is
not just that revenge is repugnant to Hamlet's moral nature, but
that he himself is not sure of the provenance of this commandment: whether it comes from Hell or Heaven. Later he considers
the possibility that 'it is a damned ghost that we have seen';[50] and
this is the same ghost to whose service he has dedicated himself.
At times he even seems to ally himself with the forces of Hell:

> 'Tis now the very witching time of night,
> When churchyards yawn, and hell itself breathes out
> Contagion to this world. Now could I drink hot blood,
> And do such bitter business as the day
> Would quake to look on.[51]

Hamlet renounces all his previous experience and all his ideals
for the sake of one commandment: in fact he gives up all that
may help him to evaluate it and adjust himself to it:

> Yea, from the table of my memory
> I'll wipe away all trivial fond records,
> All saws of books, all forms, all pressures past,
> That youth and observation copied there,
> And thy commandment all alone shall live
> Within the book and volume of my brain,
> Unmix'd with baser matter.[52]

Such a self-dedication might be appropriate for one who has seen
a vision of God: but Hamlet is not sure that he has not seen a
vision of Hell. He has been shown a crime which seems to him as
conclusive an indication of the nature of the timeless world as the
resurrection of Christ; and he has been commanded not to love,
but to hate. To Hamlet the only sign of a providence which
works behind the ordinary events of time is the dark logic of
murder and lust; the only moral imperative with which he can
ally himself is the necessity of revenge.

[50] III. ii. 80.   [51] III. ii. 378 et seq.   [52] I. v. 98 et seq.

Hamlet loses his sense of meaning. Now to Shakespeare the problem of meaning is always an interesting one. In *Love's Labour's Lost* he lightheartedly investigates the relationship (and lack of it!) between the words of love and love itself. In *Richard II* the gap between the words and the reality of kingship is explored ('Arm, arm, my name!';[53] 'Awake, thou coward majesty!').[54] And in *Lear* the King must lose his belief in the words of love and in the trappings of the social order, and descend into a meaningless limbo before he can attain to a true conception of meaning.

To Hamlet, who has wiped away from his mind all 'trivial fond records',[55] the Ghost's story and command are the only meaning in life; all other things appear empty to him. He has, moreover, seen what lies behind the falsity of the court's smiles and fair words. Consequently he finds it difficult to accept words spoken to him, in the spirit in which they were intended, and he launches what seems to be an attack on the meanings of words themselves:

> *Guil*: The King, sir, . . . Is, in his retirement, marvellous dis-temp'red.
> *Ham*: With drink, sir?[56]

> *Ros*: Then thus she says: your behaviour hath struck her into amazement and admiration.
> *Ham*: O wonderful son, that can so stonish a mother![57]

Hamlet's puns and equivoques are small skirmishes of nuance and ambiguity. Often he is blunter, tying his enemies into knots of flattery by insolent contradictions:

> *Pol*: By th' mass, and 'tis like a camel indeed.
> *Ham*: Methinks it is like a weasel.
> *Pol*: It is back'd like a weasel.
> *Ham*: Or like a whale?[58]

> *Osr*: I thank your lordship; it is very hot.
> *Ham*: No, believe me, 'tis very cold; the wind is northerly.

---

[53] *Richard II*, III. ii. 86.
[54] Ibid., 84. The problem of meaning is examined more deeply in *Richard II*, IV. i. 292–9.
[55] I. v. 99.   [56] III. ii. 292, 293.   [57] III. ii. 317 et seq.
[58] III. ii. 368 et seq.

Osr: It is indifferent cold, my lord, indeed.
Ham: But yet methinks it is very sultry and hot for my complexion. etc.[59]

Hamlet is demonstrating not only the hypocrisy of the court, but also his own loss of faith in words. He is able to stand them absurdly on their heads:

Queen: Hamlet, thou hast thy father much offended.
Ham: Mother, you have my father much offended.[60]

Hamlet's flippancy and understatement denote a breakdown of communication with other people; they also indicate the remoteness of words from the realities he has seen and is experiencing within himself. When Hamlet does talk about reality he sets himself at one remove from it and becomes incapable of action. In a sense *Hamlet* is a sort of 'anti-play'; a play works by means of words: words are what prevent this play from working. It is significant that once Hamlet becomes capable of action, he stops talking to himself and begins communicating with others. It is Laertes and Claudius who make mental reservations, not Hamlet. Hamlet gets on with the play and stops talking to the audience: yet surely it is the great soliloquies that are the heart of the play !

The loss of the sense of meaning in Hamlet points to other effects on him of his experience. Perhaps meaning is related to purpose, to the ends for which we speak and act. If we ask 'what is the meaning of an act?', what we really mean is 'what is its end?' Hamlet's misunderstandings are not a failure of comprehension of the dictionary sense of words, but of the end or intention behind them. And to Hamlet the only end of all his actions and words, in both senses of the word 'end', must be vengeance for a crime which has made all actions and words meaningless. Hamlet has dedicated his life to an end which he does not desire. A man's ideal state is perhaps a conjunction of wish and conscience; of desire and will. But Hamlet has become incapable of desire, because what he feels he should desire is repugnant to him; and to act without desire is the most spiritually exhausting thing in the world.

---

[59] v. ii. 94 et seq.   [60] III. iv. 9, 10.

Meaning, moreover, must be 'cashed' or validated by experience; and Hamlet has no experiential grounds for trust either in the world of time or in that of the timeless. A senseless world might be given meaning by a noble order in Heaven; but the other world is to Hamlet only a chaos or an ambiguity. Consequently *this* world is to him 'an unweeded garden';[61] 'this goodly frame, the earth' a 'sterile promontory';[62] the sky a 'foul and pestilent congregation of vapours';[63] Man himself a 'quintessence of dust'.[64]

For Hamlet, there is no way out: no virtues he can pursue or values he can rely on. In a curious way, he loses interest in the world: he becomes a solipsist. He talks about himself incessantly. He cannot act because he has no interest (or no 'interests') in the world he must act in; he has paralysed himself by his own too-exclusive dedication to the action of revenge, which leaves him, as it were, with no foothold in the sphere in which the action must take place. He is sad and horrified; but not angry, like Laertes: anger requires interest, and one cannot be interested in a world which seems meaningless. Hamlet has any number of potential *causes* for action: but no real motives, no inner springs of action. The time is out of joint: but Hamlet has no substantial desire to set it right.

Hamlet makes two different attempts to surmount this impasse in his nature. His first recourse is to try to stimulate in himself the emotions which he knows he lacks and which are necessary to fulfil his revenge. He takes his cue from the First Player:

> What's Hecuba to him or he to Hecuba,
> That he should weep for her? What would he do,
> Had he the motive and the cue for passion
> That I have?[65]

Perhaps by acting out a fake rage he can generate a real one:

> ... Bloody, bawdy villain!
> Remorseless, treacherous, lecherous, kindless villain!
> O vengeance![66]

---

[61] I. ii. 135.   [62] II. ii. 297.   [63] II. ii. 301.
[64] II. ii. 307.   [65] II. ii. 552 et seq.   [66] II. ii. 575 et seq.

Unlike Laertes, who is convinced by his own rhetoric, Hamlet cannot take this rant seriously. He has become like an inhabitant of another world, oddly *dégagé* from the normal interests and obsessions of life; later he even delegates to the players the performance of an unreal version of his own motives for revenge.

Unable to respond like a human being, he attempts to identify himself with the Ghost, to see himself as a Fury, an avenging angel, or a ghoul: 'Now could I drink hot blood . . .' But there is no compelling or constraining of that timeless and potent sense of wrath that can make us act like an instrument of fate. For him, power can only come from a belief in the value of actions and words—and he has lost this belief. Neither man nor ghost, he becomes wretchedly divided:

> I will speak daggers to her, but use none.
> My tongue and soul in this be hypocrites—
> How in my words somever she be shent,
> To give them seals never, my soul, consent! [67]

Having worked himself up towards action, he shies away from it and places his trust in words, which he has already found unreliable. It is not surprising that he misses his chance to kill Claudius while he is praying; nor is he able to give himself the consoling excuse of a tender conscience.

Hamlet's other attempt to resolve his paralysis is by taking refuge in the intellect. Man's reason, it seems to him, is tainted neither by the evil reality around him nor by the nightmares that lie beneath its surface. As soon as the Ghost has disappeared Hamlet attempts to cushion his mind with a kind of desperate wittiness.

> Hic et ubique? Then we'll shift our ground. [68]

> Well said, old mole! Canst work i' th' earth so fast? [96]

In the scenes that follow we see him reading a book, bewildering Polonius with a series of clever conceits, and indulging in undergraduate wit with his university friends, Rosencrantz and Guildenstern—all in the same flippant, intellectual, and superficially lighthearted tone. As soon as Hamlet realizes the folly of

---

[67] III. ii. 386 et seq.   [68] I. v. 156.   [69] I. v. 162.

trying to rouse himself to action by an emotional rhetoric, he
cudgels his mind for an intellectual solution to his problems:

> ... About, my brains. Hum—I have heard
> That guilty creatures, sitting at a play,
> Have by the very cunning of the scene
> Been struck so to the soul that presently
> They have proclaim'd their malefactions ...[70]

A play, like a philosophical argument, can contain and render
harmless, without solving, problems which can otherwise disturb
us. Hamlet is trying to externalize his problem and so get it out
of his system. Perhaps, if his plan is successful, the obvious guilt
of the spectators will make his revenge automatic, like
Hieronymo's,[71] and no longer a matter of spiritual capability. An
argument or a play is a kind of explanation—and we do not fear
what we can explain. Unfortunately, however, as always in life,
once a thing becomes intellectually compassable, it loses for us
something of its reality; and Hamlet is too honest not to realize
that his arguments and his play do not really get to grips with
his problem.

In Hamlet's soliloquy on the army of Fortinbras the advan-
tages and drawbacks of Hamlet's escape into reason are clear:

> ... What is a man,
> If his chief good and market of his time
> Be but to sleep and feed? A beast, no more!
> Sure he that made us with such large discourse,
> *Looking before and after*, gave us not
> That capability and godlike reason
> To fust in us unus'd.[72] (My italics.)

Reason raises us above the beasts of the temporal world; but contained in this speech is its flaw. Reason itself is subject to temporal considerations: it 'looks before and after', and cannot act
to change the course of time for the better. The army which
Hamlet had at first despised as irrational in its purpose becomes
the object of his admiration: it possesses at least the power of

[70] II. ii. 584 et seq.   [71] In Thomas Kyd's *Spanish Tragedy*.
[72] IV. iv. 33 et seq.

action. Reason does not contain that unreasonable sense of value that can spur on Fortinbras to great deeds:

> Witness this army, of such mass and charge,
> Led by a delicate and tender prince,
> Whose spirit, with divine ambition puff'd,
> Makes mouths at the invisible event,
> Exposing what is mortal and unsure
> To all that fortune, death, and danger, dare,
> Even for an egg-shell.[73]

Hamlet thinks 'too precisely on th' event';[74] Fortinbras 'makes mouths at the invisible event'. Reason looks before and after; Fortinbras' spirit does not weigh past and future, and is thus able to act for the sake of an 'egg-shell'. Hamlet knows this very well; but knowledge cannot help:

> And thus the native hue of resolution
> Is sicklied o'er with the pale cast of thought,
> And enterprises of great pitch and moment,
> With this regard, their currents turn awry,
> And lose the name of action.[75]

It is ironic that the very instruments Hamlet uses to stir himself to action are partially the cause of his paralysis.

Hamlet is trapped in time: quite literally, in fact; several months go by, and he has not carried out his revenge. Time is the medium of action; and action is limited by the bounds of time. The command of revenge and implications of its source seem to require an action which is timeless, which will destroy not only an individual evil but Evil itself. But he must carry out this action in the temporal world. This is the paradox: the paradox of simple capability. The word 'capable' is important in *Hamlet*:

> His form and cause conjoin'd, preaching to stones,
> Would make them capable.[76]

> That capability and godlike reason . . .[77]

> . . . incapable of her own distress . . [78]

---

[73] IV. iv. 47 et seq. [74] IV. iv. 41. [75] III. i. 84 et seq.
[76] III. iv. 126, 127. [77] IV. iv. 38. [78] IV. vii. 179.

The limitations of time itself constitute an incurable weakness, which makes us unable to fulfil our infinite desires or duties. As Troilus says in a far different context: 'The will is infinite, and the execution confined; . . . the desire is boundless, and the act a slave to limit.'[79] Hamlet has been presented with a vision of cosmic evil and chaos: to him his revenge is incomplete if he does not destroy this, the black heart of the crime. But such a revenge must be untainted by the order, limit, and kindness of time.

When Hamlet first meets the players he asks one of them for a favourite speech; and in this speech Shakespeare gives us a self-contained and precise image to crystallize Hamlet's state in our minds:

> ... Then senseless Ilium,
> Seeming to feel this blow, with flaming top
> Stoops to his base, and with a hideous crash
> Takes prisoner Pyrrhus' ear. For, lo! his sword,
> Which was declining on the milky head
> Of reverend Priam, seem'd i' th' air to stick.
> So, as a painted tyrant Pyrrhus stood
> And, like a neutral to his will and matter,
> Did nothing.
> But as we often see, against some storm,
> A silence in the heavens, the rack stand still,
> The bold winds speechless, and the orb below
> As hush as death, anon the dreadful thunder
> Doth rend the region; so, after Pyrrhus' pause,
> A roused vengeance sets him new-a-work.[80]

Hamlet is delayed in his revenge by a vision of universal chaos; in the midst of great change and destruction there is a curious dead lull. Hamlet's sword seems suspended in the air, neutral to his will and matter: action is cut off from motive and purpose. The image of storm is often associated by Shakespeare with change, action, and drama; here the storm is hushed.

This vision of storm-clouds is reminiscent of those passages in Shakespeare where the solid world is suddenly seen as transparent and without substance:

[79] *Troilus and Cressida*, III. ii. 78, 79.   [80] II. ii. 468 et seq.

Sometime we see a cloud that's dragonish;
A vapour sometime like a bear or lion,
A tower'd citadel, a pendent rock,
A forked mountain, or blue promontory
With trees upon't that nod unto the world
And mock our eyes with air. Thou hast seen these signs;
They are black vesper's pageants . . .
That which is now a horse, even with a thought
The rack dislimns, and makes it indistinct,
As water is in water.[81]

. . . These our actors,
As I foretold you, were all spirits, and
Are melted into air, into thin air;
And, like the baseless fabric of this vision,
The cloud-capp'd towers, the gorgeous palaces,
The solemn temples, the great globe itself,
Yea, all which it inherit, shall dissolve,
And, like this insubstantial pageant faded,
Leave not a rack behind . . .[82]

Shakespeare's use of the word 'rack', which occurs in the 'Pyrrhus' speech and in both the above passages, is interesting. Hamlet himself saw shapes in the clouds, like Antony, and perhaps he drew the same conclusion, that the physical world itself might be such a deception. When the timeless world comes close, either in glory or in chaos, the world of time seems dreary or insubstantial.

Many of the ideas which we find in the central soliloquy of the play, 'To be, or not to be . . .'[83] will now be familiar. This mysterious question covers a number of problems. The first is a philosophical question: whether being consists in action or suffering, in battle against the evils of life or in bearing them patiently. Action for Hamlet can only consist in the obeying of a command of destruction—destruction of others and of himself. If he acts, he dies: but perhaps this is the only way to *be*. If he suffers, he lives; but is this being?—when all life seems to be a compromise with evil, which opposes being.

---

[81] *Anthony and Cleopatra*, IV. xiv. 2 et seq.
[82] *The Tempest*, IV. i. 148 et seq.   [83] III. i. 56 et seq.

Hamlet's mind moves without a sign of its new direction, to a second problem, more closely formulated by his first question. It is the problem of choice—between literal being and not-being. Life is 'slings and arrows' and a 'sea of troubles': but to die, for Hamlet, is not to sleep, but to fall into a world of nightmare.

Perhaps non-existence would be preferable to continuing to carry the enormous burden of his own consciousness: but there is no way out of his own existence. Thus the choice between being and not-being has changed to a distinction between the world of time and the timeless world: between the 'whips and scorns of time' and 'the undiscovered country from whose bourn No traveller returns'. We can escape neither: Hamlet's problem must now be so to adjust himself to both that a viable form of existence may be found.

When Hamlet leaves for England he is incapable of changing either himself or his environment in order to be able to carry out his task. He has found that the inner springs of action cannot be constrained either by intellectual or emotional self-exercise. In this, indeed, Hamlet resembles Coleridge. For Coleridge in the 'Dejection Ode', the haloed moon foretells a storm in the heavens but no similar poetic storm within his soul; Hamlet has all the necessary causes and stimulants for action, but similarly can feel only Coleridge's:

> ... grief without pang, void, dark, and drear,
> A stifled, drowsy, unimpassion'd grief,
> Which finds no natural outlet, no relief,
> In word, or sigh, or tear ...[84]

Hamlet, too, looking on earth and heaven, might say:

> I see them all so excellently fair,
> I see, not feel, how beautiful they are![85]

Indeed the world is 'cold' and 'inanimate'[86] if no power issues forth from the soul to make it worth acting for.

Hamlet can only change through action; but he must change first in order to be able to act. As with the Ancient Mariner who

[84] ll. 21 et seq.   [85] ll. 37, 38.   [86] l. 51.

cannot pray nor save himself, the change must come from outside; as the Mariner puts it, some kind saint must take pity on him.

The change takes place on the sea-voyage. This may be significant: it suggests the providential aspects of the sea and of voyages in *Pericles, The Winter's Tale,* and *The Tempest*; and though there is no strong sea-imagery at this point to fix such an interpretation in our minds, perhaps this is deliberate: Shakespeare feels that the change which Hamlet undergoes is a mysterious one, and he refuses to be more explicit. Perhaps, indeed, Shakespeare knew that even his powers were unequal to the task of presenting such a spiritual conversion in dramatic terms; the emotional and intellectual struggles of the great soliloquies were comparatively easy to deal with. We shall see that Shakespeare is similarly cryptic at the turning-point of *The Winter's Tale.*[87] However this may be, Shakespeare leaves us with the image of imprisonment ('mutines in the bilboes'), a mysterious reference to a shaping divinity, and the picture of the Prince wrapped in his 'sea-gown'. The spiritual struggle is dealt with in a line and a half:

> Sir, in my heart there was a kind of fighting
> That would not let me sleep. Methought I lay
> Worse than the mutines in the bilboes. Rashly,
> And prais'd be rashness for it—let us know,
> Our indiscretion sometime serves us well,
> When our deep plots do pall; and that should learn us
> There's a divinity that shapes our ends,
> Rough-hew them how we will . . .
> . . . Up from my cabin,
> My sea-gown scarf'd about me, in the dark
> Grop'd I to find out them . . .[88]

Hamlet is in the dark, acting rashly and without discretion; out of the harsh light of his own analytical reason. Like Fortinbras, he 'makes mouths at the invisible event': his action is purified of cause and purpose, almost like the free, perfect crime of the existentialist hero. Hamlet's timeless vision and timeless

[87] See Chapter 8. [88] v. ii. 4 et seq.

pain cannot be prolonged in time as action. Therefore he finds a different basis for action—acting with, not against, the current of Time:

> If it be now, 'tis not to come; if it be not to come, it will be now; if it be not now, yet it will come—the readiness is all.[89]

Like Viola in *Twelfth Night*, who seems of all Shakespeare's characters to possess the most harmonious relationship with time, Hamlet seems to say:

> O Time, thou must untangle this, not I;
> It is too hard a knot for me t' untie![90]

Hamlet ceases to attempt to compel himself and his world into the situation of the perfect revenge: he is content to wait, to let the whirligig of time bring in his revenges. And oddly enough, Hamlet finds that, though when he had bent mind and passion to the fulfilment of his revenge, it fled away from him, now when he waits patiently, his revenge comes to him swiftly and without difficulty. The old antithesis of action and suffering has been resolved, and Hamlet's final posture of resolve might be called 'passive activity'. When he fluttered like a bird against the bars of the prison of time, he saw a terrible inconstancy in himself, and envied Horatio his acceptance of his limitations. Yet when at last he lets time and the 'king's pleasure' take him where it will, he discovers in himself suddenly a marble constancy:

> I am constant to my purposes; they follow the king's pleasure: if his fitness speaks, mine is ready now—or whensoever, provided I be so able as now.[91]

By a kind of surrender to time Hamlet becomes independent of it. He is able to act in accordance with the Ghost's timeless command, but no longer compelled to imitate the Ghost's timeless irresponsibility. He is free of the enormous moral burden of the Ghost's command, and can now find his own reasons for revenge: as simple justice to himself, as the removal of a nuisance rather than the working of a malefic order behind the world, as self-preservation rather than self-destruction:

[89] v. ii. 212, 213. [90] *Twelfth Night*, II. ii. 38, 39.
[91] v. ii. 193 et seq.

He that hath kill'd my king and whor'd my mother;
Popp'd in between th' election and my hopes;
Thrown out his angle for my proper life,
And with such coz'nage—is't not perfect conscience
To quit him with this arm? And is't not to be damn'd
To let this canker of our nature come
In further evil?[92]

Hamlet has regained a proper self-love, the self-love that exists within the integrated and balanced human personality. To act for the sake of political and personal justice, even if it is for his own benefit, is to be free from the nagging of irrelevant cause and motive, and from the weak and selfish introspection of the first four acts. In spite of Hamlet's disgust with the world, he realizes that it is his element, and that he must work within its terms of reference. The king has done him injury: he has an objective right to justice whether such is the commandment of the Ghost or not. Perhaps the little interchange with the Clown in the graveyard shows Hamlet how much a part of this world he is:

> *Ham*: How came he mad?
> *I Clo*: Faith, e'en with losing his wits.
> *Ham*: Upon what ground?
> *I Clo*: Why, here in Denmark. I have been sexton here, man and boy, thirty years.[93]

Hamlet, after all, stands on the ground of this world, and is an inhabitant, for good or ill, of Denmark. When Hamlet leaps into Ophelia's grave he is symbolically affirming his solidarity with the grave-bound world of time, and demonstrating a human loyalty to a woman who seemed to him at one time to be completely tainted by the universal crime of his mother. Hamlet is at last moved by emotion, not stirring it up in himself for some purpose. For the first time in the play he loses control and becomes sane. What has disturbed us about Hamlet is that he has been driving himself as one drives a car, with an appalling total control over himself and at the same time a total dissociation from himself. But now Hamlet is acting in a direct relationship with his world and in his own person: not mediating his contact with the outside world through a self with which he feels no sympathy. The temporal world with all its faults has become a justification for action; Hamlet has ceased to retreat subjectively from his own humanity and can act as a man.

The curious treaty which Hamlet seems to have signed with the forces of time, demands of him a complete involvement with the ephemeral and tainted, but still blessed creatures of time; in return he becomes free of past and future. Free of the past: he is no longer ridden by the enervating thought of the crime nor exhausted by the demands of a past self-dedication that would imply effort impossible for human nature. Free of the future: he is now willing to wait in ignorance, making 'mouths at the invisible event', for the opportunity for revenge, without fear or anticipation: 'Not a whit, we defy augury.'[94] Hamlet has found that freedom consists not in repudiation of his earthly nature and temporal environment, for this deprives him of the power of action; it lies rather in the embracing of the motives and limitations of his condition, their recognition, and their use. Hamlet cannot foresee the result of the fencing-bout, and he recognizes this; as a result he is able to use it for his own purposes. The old Hamlet would have weighed all the alternatives and missed his chance altogether in a fury of introspection. There is a hint of the latter here:

. . . thou wouldst not think how ill all's here about my heart . . .

—which he rejects:

. . . it is such a kind of gain-giving as would perhaps trouble a woman.[95]

Most important of all is the re-establishment of a proper relationship with Providence. Hamlet has recognized that his view of Providence is limited by his own small but terrifying experience of the other world. Earlier, Providence has seemed to him

[94] v. ii. 211
[95] v. ii. 205 et seq.

at worst a teleology of death by which all things operated according to the pattern of crime and revenge; at best a cosmic irony. We cannot miss the bitterness in

> ... Heaven hath pleas'd it so,
> To punish me with this, and this with me,
> That I must be their scourge and minister.[96]

Hamlet had renounced all temporal things in order to co-operate with this twisted idea of Providence: but had found himself incapable of bearing such a yoke. Now he seems to have accepted an idea of Providence as something whose purposes are greater and more mysterious than he is able to deduce from his experience:

> There's a divinity that shapes our ends,
> Rough-hew them how we will.

By involving himself with the world, with his own interests and his own loves, he has become able to throw off the nightmare of his subconscious reaction to that terrible experience, which coloured both the temporal and the timeless world in a chaotic blackness; and he can begin to co-operate with a beneficent providence. The birds of the air and the lilies of the field are protected by Providence because they are what they are,[97] and do not attempt to be other than what they are, as Hamlet has been doing. When Hamlet erased 'all trivial fond records' from his mind, he became inaccessible to Providence and unable to act with it, replacing it in his mind with the logic of the command of revenge. As soon as he is able to say '. . . there is a special providence in the fall of a sparrow',[98] seeing a mysterious order in humble things rather than a terribly clear order in great things, he is able to co-operate with it. Hamlet has discovered a pattern in the world which is untainted by the Ghost's command; and he has been able to separate the chaotic darkness of his own soul from the mysterious darkness of the purposes of heaven. The nightmare is not the timeless world itself but his apprehension

---

[96] III. iv. 173 et seq.
[97] The Sermon on the Mount is of great relevance here, particularly Matthew 6: 25–34.
[98] V. ii. 212.

of it. Hamlet has regained his faith; in particular his faith in
Providence as the effect on time of a beneficent timeless world.
And this faith in Providence is justified: time, which at first had
seemed disrupted by the appearance of the Ghost, and later the
stumbling-block and insurmountable limitation of his revenge,
now sweeps Hamlet into his victory with enormous momentum.
His victims are the instruments of their own destruction:

> Being thus benetted round with villainies—
> Ere I could make a prologue to my brains,
> They had begun the play.[99]

The play has at last been begun: not by Hamlet's words but
by the actions of his enemies. The revenge is successful: it eradi-
cates root and stock the evil in Elsinore and sets up what will be
a regime sanctified by the purpose of Providence. Hamlet has
been able to purge the world of the evil that made him hate it;
and has been able to obey the Ghost's command without being
destroyed by the evil which it had seemed to summon up in the
depths of his soul. Fortinbras' epitaph approves Hamlet the
successful man of action, and his end is in a blaze of ceremonial
Shakespearean glory:

> ... Let four captains
> Bear Hamlet like a soldier to the stage;
> For he was likely, had he been put on,
> To have prov'd most royal; and for his passage
> The soldier's music and the rite of war
> Speak loudly for him.[100]

Horatio's farewell to his friend makes the same equation of sleep
and death as Hamlet's tormented soliloquy: but now at last
Hamlet is at rest, and the sleep he is to sleep will hold no terrors.

> ... Good night, sweet prince,
> And flights of angels sing thee to thy rest![101]

[99] v. ii. 29 et seq.   [100] v. ii. 387 et seq.   [101] v. ii. 351, 352.

6. Tragedies of Love and Time: Romeo and Juliet; Troilus and Cressida; Othello

Romeo and Juliet, Troilus and Cressida, and *Othello* all deal with the defeat of love. In this chapter I shall be discussing the differences and similarities between the various enemies of love: in particular those which draw their force from the nature of time.

An initial distinction may help to organize these remarks, though it is too broad to offer much help with interpretation. *Romeo and Juliet* deals in large measure with the physical enemies of love; *Troilus and Cressida* with love's psychological enemies; and *Othello* with moral opponents of love.

We cannot avoid at this point the time-honoured and time-worn categories of Tragedy. Fate, we are told, brings about the downfall of the protagonist in a tragedy; or perhaps it is the individual who creates his own tragedy. I do not intend here to discuss the controversies and reconciliations that are made possible by such abstractions: save to remark that too often the critic peers into his literary microscope and sees there, as James Thurber once did, his own eye reflected and enlarged. 'Fate' is too often only the critic's own sense of the author organizing his work; the 'tragic flaw' is often the critic's attempt, having put himself in the place of the tragic hero, to explain to himself why *he* would not have so suffered, or to shield himself from a universe which might turn similarly sour on *him*. If we can say 'only the jealous, ambitious, foolish, or over-intellectual man must suffer like this' we are safe from the rack; for none of us is ever jealous, ambitious, foolish, or over-intellectual.

These dangerous categories may, however, serve as a starting-point. How does 'fate' work in these plays? How does the author bring about, in ways we can understand, the tragic situation he requires?

In *Romeo and Juliet* 'fate' seems to work by accident. The lovers have bad luck. A few minutes at the tomb would have made all the difference. We say of the catastrophe, 'O that it had been otherwise': there is nothing in the moral and psychological make-up of the lovers to lead us to suppose that it might not. The plot, which we can believe in without difficulty, makes Romeo and Juliet die. But we do not have the sense of a malignant god or a callous personified fate brooding over the action, that we have when Tess slips the letter declaring her guilt under Angel's door in *Tess of the D'Urbervilles.* The play might easily have had a happy ending: this is a large part of the pain we feel at what actually happens. Not that there are no thematic villains in the poetic world of this play; but the villains are able to get a grasp on the tragic protagonists in a way which is fortuitous; the tragedy would not necessarily happen again in the same circumstances. Iago will use another trap if the stratagem of the handkerchief does not present itself; 'any man' may 'sing' Cressida, 'if he can take her cliff';[1] but if Friar John had not been prevented from going to Mantua, if Romeo had been a few minutes late at the tomb, the tragedy would not have happened. Friar Lawrence plans to reconcile the Montagues and Capulets by the marriage of Romeo and Juliet; if society is the villain, it does not seem an unconquerable one. Nor can we blame Romeo's 'impetuosity'; when Tybalt taunts him, he keeps his temper; and the killing of Tybalt, which is one of the events that produce the tragedy, is forced on Romeo through no fault of his own. The blame for setting the destructive forces of time and social stupidity in motion rests with the dramatist himself, creating coincidences and arranging accidents.

Given the psychology of the central characters, however, *Troilus and Cressida* could have ended in no other way than it did. Part of the energy of this play is that people act deterministically, like machines. 'Well, well, 'tis done, 'tis past',[2] says Cressida. Time has only one direction: the end of the play results from the psychological data of the beginning. There is no way out, no spiritual freedom that might challenge the dictatorship

---

[1] *Troilus and Cressida*, v. ii. 11.   [2] Ibid., v. ii. 96.

of cause and effect in the human psyche. Troilus, for all his idealism, acts according to the plans of Pandarus; Cressida, for all her
vows, validates the cynicism of Thersites. Hector knows better
than to fight a war for a whore; but this knowledge has no hold
on him; his 'dignity' is at stake. On the Greek side, men become
machines. Achilles is an 'engine';[3] he and Ajax consider themselves the 'ram that batters down the wall';[4] Ulysses and Nestor
use them as 'draught oxen'.[5] The fall of Troy was of old one of
the 'triumphs of time': in this play the laws of time rule over all
the action:

> Yond towers, whose wanton tops do buss the clouds,
> Must kiss their own feet.[6]

> The end crowns all;
> And that old common arbitrator, Time,
> Will one day end it.[7]

> What's past and what's to come is strew'd with husks
> And formless ruin of oblivion.[8]

> And linger not our sure destructions on.[9]

In *Othello* 'fate' works in yet another way. It stems from evil
moral choice: Iago decides to destroy Othello; Othello chooses
to put his faith in Iago rather than Desdemona. 'The pity of it',[10]
we say with Othello: not 'Would it were otherwise', for it cannot
be otherwise given such moral decisions as set the play in motion;
nor do we say ''tis past, 'tis done'; for the catastrophe depended
not just on the ruthless working of the laws of time, but also on
the self-condemnation of a free man to moral imprisonment.
Though the handkerchief is a trivial and perhaps fortuitous
instrument of Iago's hatred, it is only one of many that he might
have used: we sense an irresistible current, like that of Othello's
'Pontic sea',[11] drawing us towards the scene in the bedchamber.

The categories with which we began, of 'fate' and the 'tragic
flaw', seem to come down to a distinction between the dramatic
world which destroys the individual, and the individual or
individuals who are destroyed. In each of these plays the role of

---

[3] Ibid., II. iii. 130.   [4] Ibid., I. iii. 206.   [5] Ibid., II. i. 103.
[6] Ibid., IV. v. 220–1.   [7] Ibid., IV. v. 225 et seq.   [8] Ibid., IV. v. 166.
[9] Ibid., V. x. 9.   [10] *Othello*, IV. i. 191.   [11] Ibid., 111. iii. 457.

the individual in his tragedy is different, as is the role of 'fate'. An examination of their differences within the context of this study may help to isolate their special character, and at the same time lead on to a discussion of their similarities.

In *Romeo and Juliet* the lovers are treated as 'things' by their society; as social units or as objects of attraction or gain. In order that Romeo be cured of his love-sickness for Rosaline, Benvolio invites him to attend the Capulets' feast so that he may compare his beloved with the other ladies there.

> Go thither, and with unattainted eye
> Compare her face with some that I shall show . . .[12]

Capulet asks Paris to pick out from the beauties at the feast the one he likes best; like a merchant displaying his wares:

> Hear all, all see,
> And like her most whose merit most shall be;
> Which on more view of many, mine, being one,
> May stand in number, though in reck'ning none.[13]

Lady Capulet, too, invites Juliet to examine Paris in much the same way.[14] The Nurse comforts Juliet for the banishment of Romeo by the observation that there are plenty of other fish in the sea. Why not make do with Paris? 'Wherefore', asks Juliet of Romeo, 'art thou Romeo?';[15] it is his name, his family, his classification, his status as a social unit, not as a person, which are dangerous. Yet one cannot compare persons; one can only compare things; or rather, to the extent that persons *are* things, to that extent are they comparable. Finally, of course, accident and society *do* turn the lovers into things: dead bodies.

In *Troilus and Cressida*, appetite is one of the most important factors in the movement of the plot. To yield to appetite is to make oneself into a thing; here it is not society reifying the individual, but the individual reifying himself. Troilus in III. ii, waiting for Cressida to appear, refers constantly to the physical effects of desire on his body; it is tremendously effective, but contains little or nothing of the trans-sensual ecstasy of love in

---

[12] *Romeo and Juliet*, I. ii. 85–6. [13] Ibid., I. ii. 30 et seq.
[14] Ibid., I. iii. 81 et seq. [15] Ibid., II. ii. 33.

the sonnets. His is not a love that transcends sexuality, but a
sexuality so powerful that it seems to destroy or negate all other
faculties:

> ... those fields
> Where I may wallow in the lily beds ...[16]

> I am giddy; expectation whirls me round.
> Th' imaginary relish is so sweet
> That it enchants my sense; what will it be
> When that the wat'ry palate tastes indeed
> Love's thrice-repured nectar? Death, I fear me;
> Swooning destruction, or some joy too fine,
> Too subtle-potent, tun'd too sharp in sweetness,
> For the capacity of my ruder powers.
> I fear it much; and I do fear besides
> That I shall lose distinction in my joys ...[17]

> My heart beats thicker than a feverous pulse,
> And all my powers do their bestowing lose,
> Like vassalage at unawares encount'ring
> The eye of majesty.[18]

The imagery is of touch, taste, balance, and loss of balance.
These passages are reminiscent, perhaps, of the intense sense-
imagery of Orsino's false love; a distinctly Romantic feeling of
the excess of physical delight, that must be destructive, that
makes us swoon or die like Keats's Endymion:

> ... I sigh'd
> To faint once more by looking on my bliss—
> I was distracted; madly did I kiss
> The wooing arms which held me, and did give
> My eyes at once to death: but 'twas to live,
> To take in draughts of life from the gold fount ...
> ... And, at that moment, felt my body dip
> Into a warmer air: a moment more
> Our feet were soft in flowers.[19]

[16] *Troilus and Cressida*, III. ii. 11–12.
[17] Ibid., III. ii. 17 et seq.
[18] Ibid., III. ii. 35 et seq.
[19] John Keats, *Endymion*, bk. i, ll. 651 et seq.

The ecstasy of Apollo in 'Hyperion', the 'anguish' of Porphyro in 'The Eve of St. Agnes', the poet's own swooning and painful joy in the 'Ode to a Nightingale'; this negation of self through an excess of sense-delight, is central to the Romantic movement and is equally important in Shakespeare's own discussion of love. The imagery of melting, warmth, and dissolution in *Antony and Cleopatra* has the same flavour.

But as in Sonnet 129, this pleasure is subject to time, for it makes the individual into a thing rather than a person; and things come under time's jurisdiction. Cressida's unfaithfulness, described by Troilus in terms of vomit,[20] which nicely contrasts with the taste-imagery of III. ii., demonstrates the transience of such sensations. Pandarus, who has characterized the lovers in animal terms (a 'sparrow',[21] lovebirds,[22] horses[23] birds of prey[24]) is right; Troilus and Cressida become bestial in their rejection of human selfhood. Cressida's wantonness is the wantonness of an animal. It almost cannot be blamed. Troilus has treated her as an object of desire, and she has turned out to be just, and only, that.

Othello participates in his tragedy not by reifying himself, but by reifying Desdemona. There is a sense in which the lecherous and the jealous man are doing the same thing. One is doing it to himself, the other to someone else. Desdemona becomes in Othello's mind a goat, a monkey, a minx, a toad. 'O curse of marriage,' he says,

> That we can call these delicate creatures ours,
> And not their appetites ![25]

As his jealousy increases, he concentrates more and more on Desdemona's external physical characteristics, her behaviour and what can be deduced from it.[26] His remembrance of the person that she is becomes increasingly painful to him:

[20] e.g. *Troilus and Cressida*, V. ii. 156 et seq.
[21] Ibid., III. ii. 33.
[22] Ibid., III. ii. 56. ('What, billing again?').
[23] Ibid., III. ii. 43. ('We'll put you i' th' fills').
[24] Ibid., III. ii. 41, 52.
[25] *Othello*, III. iii. 273–4.
[26] Ibid., 111. iv. 33, IV. i. 26, IV. i. 42, etc.; Iago hiself uses details and invented observations of external behaviour to lead Othello into his jealousy.

'O, the world hath not a sweeter creature; she might lie by an emperor's side and command him tasks . . . I do but say what she is: so delicate with her needle, an admirable musician—O, she will sing the savageness out of a bear!—of so high and plenteous wit and invention . . . 'But yet the pity of it, Iago! O, Iago, the pity of it, Iago!'[27]

At the end Othello has turned Desdemona into a thing, a statue rather than a woman:

> Yet I'll not shed her blood,
> Nor scar that whiter skin of hers than snow
> And smooth as monumental alabaster.[28]

Othello *must* turn Desdemona into a thing, because otherwise he would not be able to believe in her unfaithfulness. It is *humanly* impossible for Desdemona to be unfaithful: therefore she must be imagined as less than human. Further: the arguments and evidence that Iago presents rely on Othello's willingness to accept the demonstrable result of a chain of reasoning, a sequence of cause and effect, rather than the uncaused and unprovable evidence of his own faith in his wife. Faith can transcend time and cause and effect; in order for Iago to be successful, Othello must be able to look at Desdemona not as a person, but as a temporal object, subject to cause and effect.

Othello's reification of Desdemona in turn produces ugly effects in himself. His own heart becomes as stone;[29] his intentions become deterministic, unchangeable, the icy current of the 'Propontic'. He uses images to describe himself which turn him into an animal, a horned beast or a toad. Having accepted the temporal claim of reason rather than the timeless claim of faith, he becomes, in turn, inaccessible to reason; will not listen to Desdemona's explanations of the loss of the handkerchief. And having made time the basis of his moral experience, he paradoxically refuses to allow himself time to clear up the whole problem by thinking about it reasonably: the moral hierarchy has been shattered in him. Furthermore, he makes some strange mistake about time itself, which we will discuss later.

---

[27] Ibid., IV. i. 179 et seq.   [28] Ibid., V. ii. 3. et seq.
[29] Ibid., IV. i. 178 et seq.

Another area in which the differences between these plays can be discussed is that of conflict, division, and sin. The word 'sin' itself is cognate with 'sunder': a discontinuity between a man's intention and his true moral nature; an alienation from himself.

In *Romeo and Juliet* the situation in this respect is relatively clear-cut. There is obviously no moral or psychological division either within or between the lovers. The Montague–Capulet feud is not reflected in the lovers' attitude to each other: in fact they repudiate it. The social division in the play is between mirror-images: there are no profound distinctions being made by means of it. It is the fact of social conflict, the invidious division of humanity into 'us' and 'them' when there is no rational basis for such a division, which is important. The logic of such splits goes thus: 'Romeo is a Montague; Montagues are a different clan from Capulets; if they are a different clan, they are a different sort of people; the Capulets, by my experience, are human, noble, and dear; therefore if the Montagues are different, then they cannot be so; therefore they must be wicked. Therefore Romeo must be wicked, as he is a Montague'; an attempt all too universal, to resolve the aching paradox that each man is ultimately alone, that each man is 'the other' to the other, by means of a ganging-up, a blinding of oneself to one's personal differences from the other members of one's clan or nation, by an emphasis on the differences of another group from one's own.[30] This social division causes the physical separation of the lovers, and is reconciled by their death. Such divisions are based on the rationale of objectivity, and are ossified by time. A social institution (clan, state, or nation) often exists only to perpetuate itself, to preserve itself from the dangers of free choice in the changing world of time; to protect from subjectivity the individuals of which it is composed, by an easy and objective laying-down of dividing lines. It is the older generation, in whom time has worked its 'fixing' process, who crucify the younger generation in this play; the younger generation who have not yet come under the pressures of time.

[30] For an interesting analysis of this apparently universal social mechanism, see R. D. Laing, *The Politics of Experience*, 1967, chapter iv.

In *Troilus and Cressida* the division is profounder, more philosophical, psychological, and symbolic. The two camps are divided not by their mistrust of each other, but by complete differences in *Weltanschauung*. Shakespeare seems to have tugged apart two normally integral sides of human and social nature, and set them at war with each other. The differences between the Trojans and the Greeks are real, not imaginary. Most of the characters in this play are caricatures, because they each present only one or two aspects of the human totality. The imagery of division is a constant undertone:

> ... my heart
> As wedged with a sigh, would rive in twain ...[31]

> Between our Ilium and where she resides
> Let it be call'd the wild and wand'ring flood.[32]

(an image which recurs later: it is the sea, one of Shakespeare's profoundest images of time, which comes between the lovers)

> Even so
> Doth valour's show and valour's worth divide
> In storms of fortune.[33]

> Frights, changes, horrors,
> Divert and crack, rend and deracinate,
> The unity and married calm of states ...[34]

All the better; their fraction is more our wish than their faction. But it was a strong composure a fool could disunite![35]

> Let Mars divide eternity in twain
> And give him half ...[36]

> O madness of discourse,
> That cause sets up with and against itself!
> Bifold authority! ...
> Within my soul there doth conduce a fight
> Of this strange nature, that a thing inseparate
> Divides more wider than the sky and earth ...[37]

[31] *Troilus and Cressida*, I. i. 34–5. [32] Ibid., I. i. 100–1.
[33] Ibid., I. iii. 15 et seq. [34] Ibid., I. iii. 98 et seq.
[35] Ibid., II. iii. 94 et seq. [36] Ibid., II. iii. 239–40.
[37] Ibid., V. ii. 140 et seq.

This profound splitting in the play operates in a highly complex fashion. The primary division is between the Trojans and the Greeks. The Trojans are on the whole chivalric, Medieval, idealistic, honourable, romantic, intuitive, emotional, effeminate, self-abandoning and submissive in love; believing in infinites of love and honour. The Greeks tend towards a more Renaissance viewpoint; they are expedient, realistic, rationalist, reasonable (in a narrow sense), masculine, self-centred; overmastering rather than gentle; believing in the finite, the physical and possible, as opposed to the Trojan values of magnanimity and transcendence. I am generalizing broadly here, of course; and the qualities I have named, when untempered by their controls and opposites, as in this play, have lost their purity and degenerated into various forms of weakness and impotence.

Troilus and Cressida is in many ways Shakespeare's most diagrammatic and theoretical play. Those early comedies in which he manipulates various symmetries of plot are in a curious way parallel to *Troilus and Cressida*: but here the symmetries and machinery are those of faculty psychology and dramatic structure. (As in the early comedies we feel that Shakespeare dispensed with the decisiveness of his moral vision. The symmetry he has created requires the sort of moral impartiality that is normally associated with the comic or satiric modes, and is rather disturbing here.)

The primary split has resulted in a degeneration on both sides. On the Trojan side idealism and honour become ridiculous, unrelated to the facts of the situation. 'What's aught but as 'tis valued?'[38] asks Troilus:

> She is a theme of honour and renown,
> A spur to valiant and magnanimous deeds,
> Whose present courage may beat down our foes,
> And fame in time to come canonize us . . [39]

Honour and fame have always been attempts to cheat time of its prey: but they always fail of this purpose in Shakespeare. 'Time hath . . . a wallet at his back, Wherein he puts alms for oblivion.'[40]

---

[38] *Troilus and Cressida*. II. ii. 52.   [39] Ibid., II. ii. 199.
[40] Ibid., III. iii. 145, 146.

And after all, the argument is only a 'cuckold' and a 'whore'.[41] The Trojans' attempt to transcend or nullify time is doomed: '... that old common arbitrator, Time, Will one day end it'.[42] The emotional and intuitive side of the Trojans becomes a kind of sentimentality. Again and again, in II. ii, a scene heavy with the vocabulary of faculty psychology, Troilus asserts the primacy of will over wit, spirit over commonsense. Sentimentality can be defined as a disproportion between feeling and its object: this is precisely what Troilus advocates.

The Trojan submissiveness, self-abandon, and femininity become effeminacy and lechery in Paris, silliness and luxury in Troilus. The Trojan emphasis on infinitude—'the past-proportion of his infinite'[43]—becomes impracticality and impotence: '... the will is infiinite, and the execution confin'd; ... the desire is boundless, and the act a slave to limit.'[44]

On the Greek side something even more complex has taken place. If the proper precedence of the faculties is reason; will; action; if the Trojans possess 'will' in all its senses but not much of anything else; then the Greeks have the other major faculties, 'reason' and the power of 'action'. On the Trojan side are the wilful young men; on the Greek, the rationalistic leaders and the great physical brutes. A further split has now developed on the Greek side: between Agamemnon, Nestor, and Ulysses on one hand, and Ajax and Achilles on the other:

> So that the ram that batters down the wall ...
> ... They place before his hand that made the engine.[45]

And again the qualities of the Greeks degenerate. The Greek sense of policy becomes a manipulative expediency; their realism becomes cynicism (epitomized in Thersites); their reasonableness becomes an absence of the sense of honour, as when Achilles betrays Hector; their rationalism a negation of magnanimity. Their masculinity becomes homosexuality (Patroclus is Achilles' 'masculine whore');[46] their overmastering self-centredness becomes a domineering selfishness. Their emphasis on the physical becomes brutishness (Ajax 'wears his wit in his belly and his guts

41 Ibid., II. iii. 68.   42 Ibid., IV. v. 225–6.   43 Ibid., II. ii. 29.
44 Ibid., III. ii. 79–80.   45 Ibid., I. iii. 206 et seq.   46 Ibid., V. i. 16.

in his head');[47] their belief in the possible becomes a temporal determinism, so that they are subjected to cause and effect, and can be manipulated by each other; and they become the agents of cause and effect in the destruction of Troy. If the Trojan *Weltanschauung* is based on an attempt to nullify the evil forces of time through honour and love, which fails; the Greek is based on a surrender to or alliance with these destructive and inhuman forces.

The splits in what one might call the society of this play are repeated in the individual. Ajax is half-Greek, half-Trojan: there is even an image of his being divided limb from limb into his two halves. The play itself is like Ajax, irreparably divided, immensely powerful, and devoid of anything that we can admire without reserve. Achilles is a good example of such divisions:

> ... 'twixt his mental and his active parts
> Kingdom'd Achilles in commotion rages,
> And batters down himself.[48]

Troilus himself is metaphorically split in two when he perceives the treachery of Cressida.

In *Othello* the polarization is moral, not psychological. The motive force is change, or drama; rather than pattern, or the playing-out of pre-arranged psychological data. In *Troilus and Cressida* morality is not internally relevant. Everybody is morally a shade of grey. In *Othello* things are literally 'black and white'. We know where the villain is. The heroine is spotless. The hero changes dramatically and observably from a morally great man to a morally small man. Part of the problem for the critics[49] is that the change is so total and decisive. F. R. Leavis and A. P. Rossiter try to make Othello's change 'believable' by attributing to him flaws in his character which aren't there. Leavis makes Shakespeare's poetry into the villain: surely anyone who speaks

[47] *Troilus and Cressida*, II. i. 71.
[48] Ibid., II. iii. 169 et seq.
[49] F. R. Leavis, *The Common Pursuit*, 1952, 'Diabolic Intellect and the Noble Hero', p. 136; A. P. Rossiter, *Angel with Horns*, 1961, chapter 10; A. C. Bradley, *Shakepearean Tragedy*, 1915, Lecture V; J. Middleton Murry, *Shakespeare*, 1965; E. E. Stoll, 'Source and Motive in *Macbeth* and *Othello*', *Review of English Studies*, xix (1943), 25; J. I. M. Stewart, *Character and Motive in Shakespeare*, 1949, chapter v; Arthur Sewell, *Character and Society in Shakespeare*, 1951.

as magnificently as Othello does, must be self-deluded. A. C. Bradley and J. Middleton Murry play down the corrupting of Othello's mind, his wickedness after his fall. E. E. Stoll ingeniously attributes the change to dramatic necessities. It is J. I. M. Stewart and Arthur Sewell who, though opposed, seem to me to come nearest the truth. This play is about the simplest and profoundest things of all: good and evil. To attempt to explain away or to elicit a series of causal steps towards an evil action is to deny responsibility and to deny the terrible burden of moral freedom. Milton fails in *Paradise Lost*, as William Empson points out, precisely because he made the Fall 'believable': as the result of cause and effect, as steps in an argument.

The division is between moral good and moral evil. And choice here is pre-rational, taken in a sphere to which cause and effect are irrelevant. An evil choice may indeed subject an individual to a deterministic process: but this is secondary to the free choice that destroys freedom.

Othello has no psychological divisions or vacuums in him. He is a total individual, and he goes totally wrong. He chooses to believe in Iago rather than Desdemona. We should not ask 'why' this happens: we can believe it on stage (though this is painful), and our questions should, perhaps, address the 'how' and the 'wherein' of this problem. How does the sort of man Othello is morally characterize his action? Wherein does he fall? These questions will be dealt with later.

These three plays differ, finally, in the way in which time acts as the destroyer of love. In Romeo and Juliet time is a physical destroyer; its edge or point is coincidence. Caroline Spurgeon[50] and Wolfgang Clemen[51] have pointed out the imagery of light and fire, the snuffing-out of light and the choking of fire. In this play these are images of the destruction of the brief, bright human moment by time:

> Too like the lightning, which doth cease to be
> Ere one can say 'It lightens'.[52]

[50] Caroline F. E. Spurgeon, *Shakespeare's Imagery*, 1966.
[51] Wolfgang H. Clemen, *The Development of Shakespeare's Imagery*, 1951.
[52] *Romeo and Juliet*, II. ii. 119–20.

Rom: ... But come what sorrow can,
It cannot countervail the exchange of joy
That one short minute gives me in her sight.
Do thou but close our hands with holy words,
Then love-devouring death do what he dare;
It is enough I may but call her mine.
Friar L: These violent delights have violent ends,
And in their triumph die; like fire and powder,
Which, as they kiss, consume ...'[53]

> Uncomfortable time, why cam'st thou now
> To murder, murder our solemnity?[54]

Time as coincidence is heavily oppressive in this play. In Act IV
the approach of the day Juliet must marry Paris is mentioned ten
times. Yet though time is the villain, the deaths of Romeo and
Juliet are 'untimely', as Friar Lawrence states in v. iii, in his
summary of what has happened. From the point of view of
human time the deaths are untimely; from the point of view of
cosmic time they are merely happenings like any other.

In *Troilus and Cressida* time's assault is chiefly on faith:
faith 'to' primarily, and faith 'in' as secondary result. Time's
weapon is oblivion: all attempts at greatness, limitlessness, and
permanence are carried away by time's passage. This is stated
most clearly in Ulysses' advice to Achilles:

> Time hath, my lord, a wallet at his back,
> Wherein he puts alms for oblivion,
> A great-siz'd monster of ingratitudes.
> Those scraps are good deeds past, which are devour'd
> As fast as they are made, forgot as soon
> As done.[55]

> For Time is like a fashionable host,
> That slightly shakes his parting guest by th' hand;
> And with his arms out-stretch'd, as he would fly,
> Grasps in the comer.[56]

---

[53] *Romeo and Juliet*, II. vi. 3 et seq.
[54] Ibid., IV. v. 60–1.
[55] *Troilus and Cressida*, III. iii. 145 et seq.
[56] Ibid., III. iii. 165 et seq.

For beauty, wit,
High birth, vigour of bone, desert in service,
Love, friendship, charity, are subject all
To envious and calumniating Time.'[57]

The bitterness of this play is that morality is hardly important: Cressida's breaking of faith 'to' Troilus is not even a sin, only part of the natural process of oblivion which is time's effect in this play. The Cressida who betrays Troilus is not the same person as the one who pledged faith to him: there is no sense of the 'constant intention of a man's soul':[58] something in man that forms an unbroken arch above the fluctuations of time. Love, which in the Sonnets is not time's fool, is here time's subject. We are reminded of the Player King in *Hamlet*:

Most necessary 'tis that we forget
To pay ourselves what to ourselves is debt.
What to ourselves in passion we propose,
The passion ending, doth the purpose lose . . .[59]

In *Othello* time acts as a corrupter through the agency of Iago. Iago destroys Othello's faith 'in' Desdemona: Othello, by choosing to believe in Iago, ceases to believe in his wife. J. Middleton Murry says of Iago:

He . . . knows the nature of human love, and knows what accidents are necessary to destroy it.

In other words, Iago is an inevitable by-product in the process of making *drama* of the subtle tragedy of human love. Take that tragedy out of its own time-medium, and Iago is necessary to maintain its motion in the medium of the two hours' traffic of the stage. Conversely, to discover what Iago is, the time-medium must be changed back again. Then he dissolves from an incredible human being—a monster—back into his imaginative reality, which is simply the awareness of the potentiality of death in human love.'[60]

[57] Ibid., III. iii. 171 et seq.
[58] See T. S. Eliot, *Four Quartets*, 'The Dry Salvages', l. 156:
'on whatever sphere of being
The mind of a man may be intent
At the time of death'—that is the one action
(And the time of death is every moment)
Which shall fructify in the lives of others . . .
[59] *Hamlet*, III. ii. 187 et seq.
[60] J. Middleton Murry, *Shakespeare*, 1965, p. 320.

J. I. M. Stewart comments:

In Stoll's terms—or Bridges's—it comes to this: that Iago's plot can pass undetected only in the press of rapid action, but other elements in the story are plausible only if there is the contrary impression of a considerable efflux of time; and therefore Shakespeare juggles skilfully with his two clocks. But it strikes me that there is something inward about the oddity of time scheme in *Othello*. It is as if Iago only wins out because of something fundamentally treacherous in time, some flux and reflux in it which is inimical to life and love. Mr. Middleton Murry has a fine perception here when he sees that *Iago* and *time* are in some sort of imaginative balance. This is one of the things that Iago *is*: an imaginative device for making visible something in the operation of time.[61]

Iago plants in Othello's mind a temporal, unspiritual viewpoint that Othello cannot (because he does not wish to) eradicate. There is a kind of lust or attraction in us towards the purely materialistic, towards the purely temporal. C. S. Lewis describes something like this in his autobiography *Surprised by Joy*: he found science fiction unbearably and pervertedly interesting, he tells us, because it seemed to suggest ways out of our temporal predicament that were themselves temporal, that pointed away from the present towards past or future, or towards distant places; an escapism that avoided the responsibilities of spirituality. T. S. Eliot says much the same thing of our obsessions with prognostication, psychology, and evolution:

> Man's curiosity searches past and future
> And clings to that dimension. But to apprehend
> The point of intersection of the timeless
> With time, is an occupation for the saint . . .[62]

Such a fascination with the temporally explicable, the easy, mechanistic, behaviouristic view of human motivation, is a common characteristic of those who possess great idealisms and a large spiritual sense of themselves. Arthur Sewell makes some penetrating remarks about *Othello*:

There is, however, a significant separateness of 'worlds' in *Othello*; it is the separateness of Othello's world from that to which all the

---

[61] J. I. M. Stewart, *Character and Motive in Shakespeare*, 1949, p. 107.
[62] *Four Quartets*, 'The Dry Salvages', ll. 199 et seq.

other characters equally belong. In an earlier section I pointed out the difference between Othello's world and Iago's. It must now be suggested that Iago's world is the world of Venice, to which all the Venetians were born and in which they were imagined. It is more than that. It is society as Shakespeare now presented it. The central recommendation of society, so conceived, is cynically summed up in Iago's 'put money in thy purse'. It is a world in which soldiers compete for office and prestige. It is a world in which, as Emilia well knows, men will do each other's offices in the women's beds. It is a world in which lust flaunts its finery and is not abashed. It is a world, indeed, from which spirit has been drained, and all is measured by use and entertainment and position. It is a kingdom of means, not ends.

We do not judge this society by any standard to which any actual society might attain. We do not set against it an ideal society towards which an actual society might asymptotically move. In judging the society in this Venice, we make a judgment on the very nature of all society whatsoever. We see that this society is, in fact, representative of society in general; and that society in general sets up use against value, expediency against integrity, prestige against principle, behaviour against moral being. In *Othello*, two worlds are set in opposition: the world set in time and inhabited by the Venetians; the world of the spirit, in terms of which we apprehend Othello.[63]

I cannot agree with Sewell in his universal condemnation of all the Venetians (including Desdemona); but his sketch of the 'two worlds' does accord with our impressions of the relationship between Othello and Iago. Othello's para-temporal or spiritual viewpoint is indeed blinded and corrupted by Iago's evocation of temporal and materialistic 'commonsense'. But we can go further. The double time-scheme in *Othello* has often been noted.[64] Othello's jealous passion seems to us to be of such force that we cannot imagine it lasting more than a few days. All things possess a temporal decorum, a certain rhythm or amplitude that is necessary to contain them. A love-affair cannot in decency take less than a few days; a journey, if we feel it to be a journey, must take at least a few hours. Planck and Einstein tell us that electrons and universes work in certain quantum-levels

---

[63] Arthur Sewell, *Character and Society in Shakespeare*, 1951, pp. 93–4.
[64] e.g. by Kenneth Muir, *Writers and their Work*, no. 133, 1961, pp. 17–18.

of time and space. A sound is not a sound if it is measured over a short enough time. A stranger to Britain has no conception of its seasons until he has been there long enough and their rhythm has been, for him, established.

Similarly Iago's temptation of Othello implies a history of love and unfaithfulness. We know that Othello is convinced when he exaggerates impossibly to the effect that Desdemona has committed 'the act of shame' 'a thousand times',[65] which in practical terms would require at least a year!

Iago's rhythm destroys Othello's. One time-scheme upsets the other. This is at the bottom of that disturbing sense of tension we feel at a performance of this play. Our time-sense has been profoundly and subliminally disorganized. Othello's occupation's gone when Iago's sense of time has become his own. The Moor thinks in terms of values, which are perceived in an instant or which exist in a man's mind without alteration from the years. Iago thinks in terms of causality and logic, which depend on time:

> There are many events in the womb of time which will be delivered.[66]

> And wit depends on dilatory time.[67]
> Thou knows't we work by wit, and not by witchcraft;

Othello, on the other hand, wishes time might stand still at the high point of his felicity with Desdemona:

> ... If it were now to die,
> 'Twere now to be most happy; for I fear
> My soul hath her content so absolute
> That not another comfort like to this
> Succeeds in unknown fate.[68]

The Moor's superlatives and his evocation of absolutes contrast with Iago's perpetual comparatives and moral relativity. Othello genially brushes aside Desdemona's attitude to time, which avoids his own dangerous idealism as well as Iago's materialism,

---

[65] *Othello*, v. ii. 214, 215.
[66] Ibid., 1. iii. 366.   [67] Ibid., II. iii. 360-1.
[68] Ibid., II. i. 187 et seq.

and which agrees with that constructive accommodation one can make with time which we have seen in the comedies:

> *Des*: The heavens forbid
> But that our loves and comforts should increase
> Even as our days do grow!
> *Oth*: Amen to that, sweet powers!
> I cannot speak enough of this content;
> It stops me here; it is too much of joy...[69]

He continues on the subject of his timeless 'content', saying only 'amen' to Desdemona's more practical wisdom of growth.

At this point a musical image enters the poetry. Othello kisses Desdemona:

> ... this, and this, the greatest discords be
> That e'er our hearts shall make![70]

This image is full of foreboding. When there are two musics, two rhythms, two time-schemes in opposition to each other, then discord results. Iago comments:

> O, you are well tun'd now!
> But I'll set down the pegs that make this music,
> As honest as I am.[71]

Shortly afterwards, Othello sends the Clown to tell the musicians to cease the music they are playing in honour of Othello's nuptials.[72] Shakespeare uses in his stagecraft the curiously strong effect of music being broken off as a concrete analogy for what will happen to Othello's marriage. The instruments fade into silence: the music of Othello and Desdemona is stilled. Now Othello will operate to Iago's tune:

> *Des*: ... My advocation is not now in tune...[73]
>
> *Iago*: ... But yet keep time in all.[74]

—Iago's time! Othello remembers with nostalgia the music of Desdemona:

> O, she will sing the savageness out of a bear![75]

[69] Ibid., II. i. 191 et seq.
[70] Ibid., II i 196 7.
[71] Ibid,, II i 197 et seq.
[72] Ibid., III. i.
[73] Ibid., III. iv. 124.
[74] Ibid., IV. i. 92.
[75] Ibid., IV. i. 184.

His nature wrangles 'with inferior things, Though great ones' are its 'object';[76] his mighty harmony has been disrupted by Iago's miserable little jingle.

This musical image is also of great importance in the other two plays under consideration. In its clearest and simplest form it appears in *Romeo and Juliet*, when the musicians are stilled, and the marriage-feast is rudely cancelled; the ending of music portends the untimeliness and disharmony of the lovers' fates and is an analogy of the effect of coincidental time in this play, which cuts down the lovers before their time.

> *Pet*: O play me some merry dump to comfort me.
> *1 Mus*: Not a dump we! 'Tis no time to play now.[77]

In *Troilus and Cressida*, too, music is an important image. There is discord in both camps:

> Take but degree away, untune that string,
> And hark what discord follows![78]

> *Pan*: ... Fair prince, here is good broken music.
> *Par*: You have broke it, cousin; and by my life, you shall make it whole again; you shall piece it out with a piece of your own performance.
> *Helen*: He is full of harmony.
> *Pan*: Truly, lady, no.
> *Helen*: O, sir—
> *Pan*: Rude, in sooth; in good sooth, very rude.
> *Par*: Well said, my lord. Well, you say so in fits.[79]

Pandarus, if we wished to stretch this piece of badinage, might be said to be incapable of 'making whole' or 'piecing out' the 'broken' music of Troilus and Cressida in his role of pander.

Other themes that we have noted in *Othello* can be seen in its predecessors. The difference in *Weltanschauung* which exists initially between Iago and Othello (and which is horrifyingly resolved) corresponds in many ways with that between the lovers in *Romeo and Juliet* and the social world in which they live. I

---

[76] *Othello*, III. iv. 145–6.
[77] *Romeo and Juliet*, IV. v. 104 et seq.
[78] *Troilus and Cressida*, I. iii. 109–10.
[79] Ibid., III. i. 47 et seq.

think it was Coleridge who first noticed that two different kinds of imagery appear in *Romeo and Juliet*:[80] a more conceited, 'poetical' imagery, and a more organic, 'dramatic' imagery. Clemen explains this in terms of the historical development of the dramatist;[81] *Romeo and Juliet* is a play transitional between an earlier style of unconnected imagery and a later one of molecular imagery more deeply involved with the submerged thematic currents of the play. We can cite the great molecular symbol of light–fire–smoke–darkness as an example of the latter, and the 'witty' language of Capulet and of Romeo's young friends for the former. Pursuing this distinction a little further, however, it seems that it is the poetry of true love that is of the more organic kind, and that of the play's society which is of the wittier variety. On one hand we have the lovers, expressing their ecstasy and tragedy in great images that appear again and again throughout the play:

> O, speak again, bright angel, for thou art
> As glorious to this night, being o'er my head,
> As is a winged messenger of heaven
> Unto the white-upturned wond'ring eyes
> Of mortals that fall back to gaze on him,
> When he bestrides the lazy-pacing clouds,
> And sails upon the bosom of the air.[82]

On the other hand there are the rather unmemorable puns and conceits of Capulet, for instance:

> How now! a conduit, girl? What, still in tears?
> Evermore show'ring? In one little body
> Thou counterfeit'st a bark, a sea, a wind;
> For still thy eyes, which I may call the sea,
> Do ebb and flow with tears. The bark thy body is . . . etc.[83]

One great difference between these two kinds of imagery is that Romeo's is full of moral significance: it deals in values, it points to the deeper forces of joy and sorrow that underlie human action; whereas Capulet's imagery is there not to give greater

[80] In his Lecture VIII, 1811-12: '*Romeo and Juliet*'.
[81] Op. cit.
[82] *Romeo and Juliet*, II. ii. 26 et seq.
[83] Ibid., III. v. 129 et seq.

meaning to the events on stage, but to provide intellectual entertainment and to illustrate the silliness of the speaker. Romeo's
image *is* Juliet; Capulet's has nothing to do with her.

These two kinds of imagery correspond, I submit, not to two
stages in Shakespeare's development, but to two types of moral
vision in the play. The lovers deal in values, in meaning, in
realities; the other characters in uses, means, and names. The
lovers deny the conventional categories of their world when they
cry 'What's in a name?';[84] they are interested in meanings, not
words; in ends, not means. And as with all who try to live such
a creed without compromise in a world that is hostile to it, they
are doomed.

Romeo and Juliet is one of the richest fields in Shakespeare
for those who, like Eric Partridge[85] are on the hunt for bawdy
puns and innuendoes. And here again we find a distinction between the language of the lovers and that of the world they live
in. Once Romeo has deserted Rosaline (to whom almost every
reference contains some 'sallet'), his relationship with Juliet is
devoid of any such verbal impurities. Around the lovers the
Nurse, Benvolio, Mercutio and even the more respectable figures
continue to pun on sexual matters: but the lovers themselves
have risen above this sort of thing. The language of true love is
for them purged of materialism; they are no longer concerned
with the causalities of lust, the determinism of the flesh. Not that
they become asexual; *Romeo and Juliet* cannot be played on
stage without conveying a sense of the enormous sexual force of
the young lovers: but the bawdy, coarse, Iago-ish approach to
sex (the 'beast with two backs') is absent from their love. Romeo
and Juliet act towards each other as though they had both read,
and obeyed, the prescriptions of Shakespeare's Sonnets.

There is a clear contrast between the young lovers and the
older generation with respect to their attitude towards the pace
of action. The older generation are content to take things slowly;
they see action in a historical context; they realize that things will
not greatly differ in a hundred years as a result of their actions.

---

[84] *Romeo and Juliet*, II. ii. 43.
[85] Eric Partridge, *Shakespeare's Bawdy*, 1955.

Their rhythm is not the rhythm of the lovers, who regard that kind of 'realism' as an admission of defeat in the war against time, and who are frustrated by patience and method:

> The clock struck nine when I did send the nurse;
> In half an hour she promis'd to return.
> Perchance she cannot meet him—that's not so.
> O, she is lame! Love's heralds should be thoughts,
> Which ten times faster glide than the sun's beams
> Driving back shadows over louring hills;
> Therefore do nimble-pinion'd doves draw Love,
> And therefore hath the wind-swift Cupid wings.
> Now is the sun upon the highmost hill
> Of this day's journey; and from nine to twelve
> Is three long hours, yet she is not come . . .
> . . . But old folks—many feign as they were dead,
> Unwieldy, slow, heavy, and pale as lead.[86]

And there follows the comic scene of the Nurse's procrastination. The younger generation, the lovers, live feverishly fast by comparison. They attempt to negate time by making action as nearly contemporaneous with thought and feeling as possible. The older generation have a 'stake' in time; time has been the medium of their survival; but to the lovers, who have no such trust in time, the present moment is all, and their elders seem 'dead'. In an exchange between Romeo and Friar Lawrence there is much the same contrast. Lawrence is concerned with the future, and bases his judgement on experience of the past:

> So smile the heavens upon this holy act
> That after-hours with sorrow chide us not!

Romeo replies:

> Amen, amen! But come what sorrow can,
> It cannot countervail the exchange of joy
> That one short minute gives me in her sight.
> Do thou but close our hands with holy words,
> Then love-devouring death do what he dare;
> It is enough I may but call her mine.

[86] *Romeo and Juliet*, II. v. 1 et seq.

Lawrence is pessimistic:

> These violent delights have violent ends,
> And in their triumph die; like fire and powder,
> Which, as they kiss, consume . . .
> . . . Too swift arrives as tardy as too slow.[87]

We will hear similar words in the mouth of Claudius, many years later in Shakespeare's career, when he is a good deal closer to a reconciliation of these apparently opposed points of view:

> There lives within the very flame of love
> A kind of wick or snuff that will abate it;
> And nothing is at a like goodness still . . .[88]

The kind of disharmony between two different rhythms of life that we have glimpsed in *Othello* is already present in *Romeo and Juliet*.

If the lovers of Verona are able to deny and transcend the categories of lust and the conventions of materialism, the lovers of Troy accept them and so adulterate their love that it has no defence against forgetfulness. Superficially we can see many of the distinctions in this play that we have seen in *Romeo and Juliet*: the Trojan sense of value opposed to the Grecian expediency and commonsense; Troilus' vision of love as eternal, his desire that time might stand still, opposed to Ulysses' realism about 'oblivion' and the Greek sense that 'time is on their side'. In Troilus indeed, the hallmarks of the Shakespearean lover are very clear:

> To feed for aye her lamp and flames of love;
> To keep her constancy in plight and youth,
> Outliving beauty's outward, with a mind
> That doth renew swifter than blood decays![89]
>
> As true as steel, as plantage to the moon,
> As sun to day, as turtle to her mate,
> As iron to adamant, as earth to th' centre—
> . . .'As true as Troilus' shall crown up the verse
> And sanctify the numbers.[90]

---

[87] *Romeo and Juliet*, II. vi. 1 et seq.   [88] *Hamlet*, IV. vii. 114 et seq.
[89] *Troilus and Cressida*, III. ii. 156 et seq.   [90] Ibid., III. ii. 173 et seq.

Cres: Night hath been too brief.
Troi: Beshrew the witch! With venomous wights she stays
As tediously as hell, but flies the grasps of love
With wings more momentary-swift than thought.[91]

All this is familiar: the idea of constancy, outliving outward
show; the vows on the structure of the universe itself; the cursing
of time that will not stand still for love. Romeo had similarly
cursed the lark; Othello wishes that he might die at the peak of
his joy. Earlier on Troilus himself feared that the excess of joy
might even be his death—'swooning destruction'.[92] Even in
small details, such as Troilus' impatience with Pandarus in Act I,
scene i, we can see a resemblance with *Romeo and Juliet*: Juliet
is similarly teased and exasperated by the Nurse, who knows
nothing of the swiftness of love's wings. Again, in both plays
the imagery of loving birds, particularly birds of prey, is important.[93]

[91] Ibid., IV. ii. 11 et seq.
[92] Ibid., III. ii. 22.
[93] Bird-imagery is strong in all three of these plays. In *Romeo and Juliet*: to
lure this tassel-gentle back again' (II. ii. 159) etc.; there are also references to the
'wanton's bird' and to Juliet's bedchamber as a nest. In *Troilus and Cressida*: 'The
falcon as the tercel, for all the ducks i' the river' (III. ii. 51); with a possible
reference to the emblematic or allegorical significance of birds as is found in the
Parlement of Foules. In *Troilus and Cressida* there are many other references to
loving birds. The imagery of birds in *Othello* is still that of birds of prey, but
here the tone is different:
                    If I do prove her haggard,
          Though that her jesses were my dear heart-strings,
          I'd whistle her off and let her down the wind
          To prey at fortune. (III. iii. 264).
In all three plays there are allusions to the art of falconry, such as 'seeling', i.e.
hooding, and 'watching him tame', i.e. the practice of keeping a hawk awake to
make him tame.
    This use of bird-imagery in the poetry of love is part of a long tradition:
          What mighte or may the sely larke seye,
          Whan that the sperhawk hath it in his foot?
                    Geoffrey Chaucer, *Troilus and Criseyde*, III. 1191.

    And now, like am'rous birds of prey,
    Rather at once our time devour
    Than languish in his slow-chapped power.
                    Andrew Marvell, 'To His Coy Mistress', l. 38.
Anyone who has observed birds in the ecstasy of mating will recognize the force
of these images. The Argentinian ornithologist Carlos Selva Andrade writes in his
Love-Life of the Birds:

But the difference is that to attain the joyful state he celebrates, Troilus has required the services of 'bed, chamber, pander, to provide this gear';[94] he has had to compromise with Pandarus as Juliet never had to compromise with the Nurse. Cressida's raptures are genuine; but like the raptures of a drug they wear off and leave no residue. The imagery of Troilus' love is forebodingly that of appetite and digestion; of curious and compound sweets, moreover, rather than of 'simple savour'.[95] This time the conventional cynicism of a Thersites is justified; in *Romeo and Juliet* the lovers had died without compromising their idealism or justifying the cynicism of Romeo's young friends, and in *Othello*, Iago must persuade the Moor of his cynical view of the world before the betrayal can take place. Troilus' attempt at the eternal, the terminal, in love, cannot succeed; the lovers are left shivering in the dawn that must spiritually sever them forever, and Cressida may be catching cold. The 'monstruosity' of love that Troilus had proclaimed as a boast of his infinite desire and boundless will, rebounds as a description of the impossibility of a love that compromises in act and execution with lust and materialism. Ultimately there is not much difference between the attitude of Pandarus, the lovers' go-between, and that of Thersites, their

'If someone were to take, say, a sparrow's temperature, he would find that it is 111°. The most advanced homoiothermous organisms seldom exceed 98°. At 104° a human being is delirious; the habitual fever of the sparrow would be fatal.

'But the bird continuously squanders his energy; he lives for excitement. The exhausting effort of flying, the constant restlessness, the light and brief sleep neither weaken nor tire him. Consumed by an inner fire, can he logically moderate his passions?

'It is perhaps for this reason that the prolegomena of mating are more intense in these splendid creatures than in any other class of vertebrates. Each phase of the nuptial ceremony is imbued with passion. He himself is, mentally and physically, the ceremony. During the hostile delirium of love he easily reaches frenzy. Vibrant, transfigured, like an overcharged battery, he discharges his intense emotion in violent outbursts.' (Trans. from the Spanish by Herbert M. Clark, published in Buenos Aires.)

Romeo and Troilus at the peak of their passion answer this description fairly well. Love for them (as with Chaucer's Troilus and the lover of the 'Coy Mistress') is something so intense that it seems to take them out of ordinary, measured time into the time-sense of fever. Chaucer's Troilus and Criseyde, incidentally, curse the dawn and the swiftness of night just like Shakespeare's lovers.

[94] *Troilus and Cressida*, III. ii. 207.
[95] Sonnet 125.

cynical critic. Thersites says: 'If you just use your head you can see that love and honour are only bawdy and conceit'; Pandarus says: 'Never mind about love and honour. *I* know that what you are really after is a bedmate. Let's get down to basics.' The difference resembles that between Jaques and Touchstone.

The dichotomies that we have been investigating in these plays corrspond to certain distinctions we have noted in *As You Like it*, between the subjective, objective, and animal approaches to living in time. Jaques, Capulet, the Greeks, Iago, see time as history, as casual sequence. The present moment is of no more importance to them than any other moment. It is perhaps no coincidence that Jaques and Iago are the same name. Not much different, perhaps, as such figures as Touchstone, the Nurse, Pandarus, and Emilia, who appeal not to expediency (and therefore casual sequence) as a justification of action, but to the brute impulses of nature, which are similarly independent of subjectivity. In many respects this latter group has more kindness (in both the senses of this word) than the cynically objective characters; but they are no less the enemies of the subjective qualities of love, faith, honour. One's love can either be destroyed by an Iago or subtly corrupted by a well-intentioned Pandarus. In contrast are Romeo, Troilus, Othello—all three are by protestation believers in the personal judgement, the primacy of the living moment, the massive stability of the subjective decision, which, because it is not of time, 'alters not' with time's 'brief hours and weeks'.[96] Romeo stands firm, and blind incidental time is his undoing; Troilus is flawed by animality; Othello becomes objective, insane to his former lucid subjectivity.

Around the lovers are those who are part of natural time and who, like animals, cannot rise above it; who are operated on by the determinisms of time and have in themselves no source of moral autonomy; around them also are those who pull the puppet strings, who work with means and with causes, and who reject the timeless, present motions of the human spirit. In the centre of these plays are the lovers themselves, who wish that time might stand still, that the present, as Augustine put it, 'might

[96] Sonnet 116.

not pass on to become time past',[97] but might endure as eternity, the heaven of love. The tragedy is that a fourth alternative is ignored: Viola's use of time as a rhythm which will afford the moment for the spirit to be free; Hamlet's final vision of time sanctified by Providence; the sense of growth that we can see in Sonnet 115 and in Desdemona's answer to Othello's 'If it were now to die'.[98] The image of broken music, of disharmony, is of central importance here. What is lacking is the harmony of *Twelfth Night*, the music that awakens the statue in *The Winter's Tale*.

There is almost a Platonic sense of imperfection in these plays. 'Nothing is at a like goodness still';[99] the finest things contain a flaw, or consume themselves, or are swallowed up in darkness. The fire and light of *Romeo and Juliet* cannot hold their perfection, but are snuffed out. Love itself is composed of intensely postive but also equally intensely negative forces; it contains its own contradicitions:

> ...O brawling love! O loving hate!
> O anything, of nothing first create!
> O heavy lightness! Serious vanity!
> Mis-shapen chaos of well-seeming forms!
> Feather of lead, bright smoke, cold fire, sick health! ...[100]

Plato would have agreed that in this sublunary world everything contains the potentiality of its opposite, and indeed tends towards its opposite. In the world of time and mutability, perfections cannot endure. The beauty, the extremism of the love in this play is 'too rich for use, for earth too dear'.[101] The lovers call their love infinite, but in the world of time there can be nothing infinite: time itself turns against the lovers, and blindly ejects them from its system as incompatible with its texture and tissue. The lovers treat time subjectively—'For in a minute there are many days'[102] —and time revenges itself blindly for such temerity.

---

[97] Sir Tobie Matthew, Kt., trans, *The Confessions of St. Augustine*, revised and emended Dom Roger Hudleston, Orchard Books, 1954, p. 341.
[98] *Othello*, II. i. 191.
[99] *Hamlet*, IV. vii. 116.
[100] *Romeo and Juliet*, I. i. 174 et seq.
[101] Ibid., I. v. 45.　　　　　　　　　　　[102] Ibid., III. v. 45.

In *Troilus and Cressida*, too, we sense the tragedy of imperfection. Love is monstrous in that its temporal expression cannot equal its infinite aspirations: all action is 'biased'[103] like a bowl, and will not result in what was intended. The fountain of love is blemished with a 'dreg'.[104] Time proves how finite are the love and honour of Troy, which had claimed infinitude, had claimed to be 'past-proportion'.[105]

Othello is obsessed with imperfection. He imagines that he keeps 'a corner' in the things he loves 'for others' uses';[106] that Desdemona is flawed. As in *Romeo and Juliet* there is the imagery of light and darkness, of light giving way to darkness; though here the light does not snuff itself out, but is extinguished by Othello: 'Put out the light . . .'.[107] Iago is the rot or corrosion of moral perfections that usually takes years to set in, if it sets in at all. But odd things have happened to time in this play, and emotional entropy has been enormously accelerated.

These plays, then, though they differ vastly in many details and profoundly in their moral climate and structure, contain in common several basic assumptions about time and love. In them there is, if not a development away from the clear lines of the sonnets, at least an elaboration, a deepening and broadening of the theme into new moral situations. More important still: in fourteen lines life must be seen in a flash, for a moment, even if it is a moment for all time; in a play, the problems of duration and accident arise. And this can be the setting of a tragedy.

[103] *Troilus and Cressida*, I. iii. 15.   [104] Ibid., III. ii. 63.
[105] Ibid., II. ii. 29.   [106] *Othello*, III. iii. 276–7.
[107] Ibid., V. ii. 7.

7. The Crime of Macbeth

. . . they strive to have some relish of things eternal while their heart—as yet unstable withal—doth flicker to and fro in the motions of things past and to come. Who shall be able to hold and fix it, that for a while it may be still, and may catch a glimpse of Thy ever-fixed eternity, and compare it with the times that never stand, so that he may see how these things are not to be compared together? . . .[1]

. . . Thou art still the same and thy years fail not. Thy years neither go nor come; but ours do both go and come, that they may all be come in their order . . . Thy years are all one day; and thy day is not every day, but today; because thy today neither gives place to tomorrow, nor comes it in place of yesterday. Thy today is eternity . . .[2]

Those two times therefore, the time past and the time future, how are they; since the time past is now no more, and the time future is not yet come? And as for the present, if it could be for ever present and not pass on to become time past, truly it should not be time but eternity.[3]

Future things then are not yet: and if they are not yet, they have no being; and if they have no being, they cannot be seen; yet may they be foretold by means of some present things, which both are already, and are seen.[4]

Neither times past nor times future have any being.[5]

THESE quotations from the *Confessions* of St. Augustine seem to sum up the basic thinking on time, which underlay the Middle Ages and the Renaissance alike, and which helped to form the framework of assumptions and holy commonplaces on which *Macbeth* was built. On one hand there is the transitory and illusory world of past and future, which limits our perception of reality, and in which, indeed, there is no being: the world of 'tomorrow, and tomorrow, and tomorrow'; on the other hand

---

[1] Sir Tobie Matthew, Kt., trans., *The Confessions of St. Augustine*, revised and emended Dom Roger Hudleston, Orchard Books, 1954, p. 337.
[2] Ibid., p. 340. [3] Ibid., p. 341. [4] Ibid., p. 346.
[5] Ibid., p. 347.

there is the vision of the perpetual 'today' which is the milieu of
God and His Angels, of man's true destiny, and of the soul of
the just man: '. . . but these years of Thine shall all be ours, when
time shall be no more.'[6] But, says Augustine, it is our condition
that we should pass from past to future; while we live we must
accept the limitations of time, because they are part of the pattern
of God's intention, and are sanctified by a divine order: 'Thy
years neither go nor come; but ours do both go and come, that
they may all be come in their order . . . .'

The blasphemy of Macbeth is that he rebels against these
sacred and essential ordinances of creation. 'Blood hath been shed
ere now,' he says,

> . . . i' th' olden time,
> Ere human statute purg'd the gentle weal;
> Ay, and since too, murders have been perform'd
> Too terrible for the ear. The time has been
> That when the brains were out the man would die,
> And there an end; but now they rise again,
> With twenty mortal murders on their crowns,
> And push us from our stools. This is more strange
> Than such a murder is.[7]

Macbeth's crime is no ordinary murder, and he senses this, like
the chorus in *Murder in the Cathedral* who guess that the killing
of Becket is some similarly extraordinary event. The sin of
Macbeth is not merely against 'human statute', but against the
laws of creation itself. Not that Macbeth shows much moral
sensitivity to his crime: he is concerned here, as usual, with the
physical consequences of his actions and their effect on his own
interests. His tone is indignation rather than remorse; but he can
see clearly, as Hamlet sees when his father's ghost appears, that
some unnatural disturbance of the ordinary temporal world has
taken place.

Macbeth begins with a prediction. I have not used the term
'prophecy' because a prophet is a man who is able to stand outside time, and perceive the pattern of time from an eternal viewpoint: the human preoccupation with the sensational and the

temporal has transformed the word from its proper sense to the sense of mere prognostication. The Witches are closer to the cheap fortune-teller than to the man who has some knowledge of the mind of God. T. S. Eliot makes the distinction tellingly:

> To communicate with Mars, converse with spirits,
> To report the behaviour of the sea monster,
> Describe the horoscope, haruspicate or scry,
> Observe disease in signatures, evoke
> Biography from the wrinkles of the palm
> And tragedy from fingers; release omens
> By sortilege, or tea leaves, riddle the inevitable
> With playing cards, fiddle with pentagrams
> Or barbituric acids, or dissect
> The recurrent image into pre-conscious terrors—
> To explore the womb, or tomb, or dreams; all these are usual
> Pastimes and drugs, and features of the press:
> And always will be, some of them especially
> When there is distress of nations and perplexity
> Whether on the shores of Asia, or in the Edgware Road.
> Man's curiosity searches past and future
> And clings to that dimension. But to apprehend
> The point of intersection of the timeless
> With time, is an occupation for the saint . . .[8]

True, the Witches are not charlatans: but when Macbeth hears them, and later when he commands them to tell him of his future, he is 'clinging' to the 'dimension' of time past and time future; and their words do not release him from the confines of time, but bind him totally within them. Furthermore, we may infer from Augustine's statement that 'future things . . . have no being' that Macbeth's obsession with the future involves him in a shadowy world of not-being. Can it be significant that Macbeth terms the Witches' words a 'supernatural soliciting'[9] and a 'prophetic greeting'?[10] Has he already confused the intoxication of knowing something of the future with the power of timeless wisdom?

The knowledge of the Witches is not a spiritual knowledge, but a temporal knowledge. They gain it not by converse with

---

[8] 'The Dry Salvages', ll. 184 et seq.   [9] I. iii. 130.   [10] I. iii. 78.

God or with angels but from a charm involving the most physically obtrusive and material objects imaginable: 'Eye of newt, and
toe of frog' etc.[11] Their words are true in the letter but not
in the spirit. There is a correspondingly curious literalism about
Macbeth's apprehension of what the Witches tell him: he relates
everything they say to his own dynastic and political ambitions.
This attitude is shown symbolically to lead to self-destruction
by means of the appearance of the ironic literal truth of the predictions. Macbeth is traditionally a figure of supernatural and
spiritual evil: but in fact he is a person in whom the supernatural
and the spiritual are completely destroyed. That contact with the
supernatural which the Witches seem to possess suffices only to
empty Macbeth of the last vestiges of spirituality. Macbeth is not
possessed by an evil spirit, but by the determinism of pragmatic
motives and expedient policy acting on a strong imagination.

In Book II of the *Faerie Queene* Alma conducts Guyon round
her castle, the House of Temperance. This guided tour ends in a
visit to a high turret,[12] which represents allegorically the head
of the human body. The turret is divided into three rooms where
dwell 'three honourable sages', of whom

> The first . . . could things to come foresee:
> The next could of things present best aduise;
> The third things past could keepe in memoree . . .[13]

The first sage is named 'Phantastes'; and the room in which he
lives clearly represents the creations of imagination or fancy.

> His chamber was dispainted all within,
> With sundry colours, in the which were writ
> Infinite shapes of things dispersed thin;
> Some such as in the world were never yit,
> Ne can deuized be of mortall wit;
> Some daily seene, and knowen by their names,
> Such as in idle fantasies doe flit:
> Infernall Hags, Centaurs, feendes, Hippodames,
> Apes, Lions, Aegles, Owles, fooles, louers, children, Dames.[14]

---

[11] IV. i. 14.
[12] J. C. Smith, ed., Spenser's *Faerie Queene*, 1961, vol. i; Bk. III, canto IX,
stanza xliv.   [13] Ibid., III. IX. xlix.   [14] Ibid., III. IX. 1.

We can infer that Spenser identifies that human faculty which deals with the future, with the fancy or imagination.

Whether Shakespeare borrowed this idea, or whether it was an Elizabethan commonplace, he seems to use it where he deals with the Witches. The Witches are termed 'fantastical';[15] they themselves resemble Puck in their mischief[16] and in their association with strange animals,[17] and Puck is to a large extent a symbol of the imagination. Magic is closely associated with fantasy and imagination; and the Witches' function in *Macbeth* is that of prediction of the future. '. . . One of the prime objects of magic', says G. L. Kittredge on this subject, 'is to read the future.'[18]

Obviously the Witches have a real objective existence in the play. But it is equally obvious that there exists a very special relationship between Macbeth and the Witches, which can be illustrated by a comparison between the Witches' effect on Macbeth, and their lack of effect on Banquo.

In some sense Macbeth and the Witches can be said to make up an imaginative whole. We can see this in other plays: Othello and Iago, Hamlet and the Ghost, and Lear and the Fool are welded together in the same way. In psychology we are familiar with the processes of projection, indentification, and internalization. Psychologically Othello swallows the attitudes and idioms of his tempter: 'I am your own for ever',[19] says Iago. Hamlet absorbs his Ghost, Lear becomes his own Fool. Macbeth assimilates the Witches in the same way.

But plays are not just psychology: they are also drama. In drama the characters are largely created by their interactions with each other. Macbeth's relationship with the Witches is not just a psychological dependence, but also a dramatic symbiosis. Macbeth's instant and overwhelming psychological response to the Witches is verbally echoed in a dramatic repetition: 'Fair is foul, and foul is fair';[20] 'So foul and fair a day I have not seen'.[21] Psychologically Macbeth internalizes the Witches so that they

[15] I. iii. 53.   [16] e.g. *A Midsummer Night's Dream*, II. i. 42 et seq.
[17] *A Midsummer Night's Dream*, III. i. 96 et seq.
[18] G. L. Kittredge, *Witchcraft in Old and New England*, Harvard University Press, 1929, p. 226.   [19] *Othello*, III. iii. 483.
[20] I. i. 10.   [21] I. iii. 38.

become a principle of his own conduct; dramatically the Witches come to represent something in him, so that one way of finding out about Macbeth is to find out about the Witches. What the Witches say to Macbeth is in some respects what Macbeth says to himself.

The Witches deal with the future; the future is the business of the imagination. Macbeth does not imagine the Witches;[22] but the Witches represent his own imagination. Imagination proposes to him that he will rise in station, and become, for instance, Thane of Cawdor. Imagination tells him he will be King. Imagination pronounces him invulnerable to man of woman born—in other words, he can no longer be harmed by any human agency. As we shall see, this insight is curiously accurate. The image of Birnam Wood coming to Dunsinane is a paradigm of impossibility, like those in Hamlet's little poem to Ophelia.[23] The implication is that Macbeth's imaginative idea of the possible is limited by his own corruption. If one commits a crime which is morally impossible, as Macbeth does, one should not be surprised at the apparently impossible physical consequences. One cannot, in Shakespeare's view, disturb the moral structure of the universe without the possibility of a convulsion among its physical laws. Macbeth realizes this painfully when Banquo's ghost appears.

Within the context of the symbolic relationship of Macbeth with the Witches their otherwise banal and mechanical predictions gain depths of nuance and irony, displaying the intensity and, equally, the limitations of Macbeth's imagination. It is necessary for a full appreciation of the role of the Witches to keep in the mind two ways of looking at them: as real Witches whose words are invested by Macbeth's imagination with the motives for his crime, and as a symbolic crystallization of that faculty of prophetic imagination which has become corrupt in him and uncontrolled by his total personality.

[22] Theseus in *A Midsummer Night's Dream*, V. i. 18 et seq., remarks of 'strong imagination': '. . . in the night, imagining some fear, How easy is a bush suppos'd a bear!' Macbeth similarly turns three old hags into the vast, shadowy terrors of his own imagination.

[23] *Hamlet*, II. ii. 115 et seq.

Traditionally the driving force within Macbeth that motivates his crime is ambition. At first sight such an explanation seems inadequate to account for the extravagant horrors of the play. We prefer some metaphysical or psychological subtlety which will seem as impressive intellectually as the drama seems emotionally. But what exactly *is* ambition? Surely an obsession with the future, that will not allow us peace (or spiritual growth) in the present. Of the women who surround Macbeth, the Three Witches, as we have seen, arouse or represent Macbeth's imaginative obsession with the future; and Lady Macbeth's function is to stir up his intellectual and emotional fixation with what is to come:

> Thy letters have transported me beyond
> This ignorant present, and I feel now
> The future in the instant.[24]

Lady Macbeth's contempt for the present, which, as Augustine points out, is the milieu of God, is significant. The present is only there to be hoodwinked by those who have their basis in the future:

> Look like the time . . .[25]
> . . . To beguile the time,

The present is important only in relation to the future, present actions only the means to a future end:

> . . . and you shall put
> This night's great business into my dispatch;
> Which shall to all our nights and days to come
> Give solely sovereign sway and masterdom.[26]

Here we have a conception of ambition which seems adequately to account for its fearful effects. Macbeth himself elucidates its metaphysical depths in a speech whose language carries an unexpected but totally fitting impression of nervous fancifulness:

> If it were done when 'tis done, then 'twere well
> It were done quickly. If th' assassination
> Could trammel up the consequence, and catch,
> With his surcease, success; that but this blow
> Might be the be-all and the end-all here—

[24] I. v. 53 et seq.   [25] I. v. 60, 61.   [26] I. v. 64 et seq.

But here upon this bank and shoal of time—
We'd jump the life to come.[27]

Macbeth twitters with a suppressed and feverish excitement,
expressed in puns and conceits that seem not quite to express
what he means. Moreover, he is grappling with a concept of the
Hereafter that his moral condition makes him unable to compre-
hend. But it is clear what is happening: Macbeth has tied up all
his personality in the future, and cut himself off from the grace
that can only come from beyond time by way of the present
moment. In his letter to his wife he writes: 'these weird
sisters saluted me, and referr'd me to the coming on of time, with
"Hail, king that shalt be!" '.[28] From now on Macbeth is unable
to escape from the dreary and fateful 'coming on of time'. Such
is the nature and result of 'vaulting ambition, which o'er-leaps
itself'.[29]

Macbeth is now firmly in the grip of his imaginative obsession with the future. He commits his crime—the scene is
described with exquisite critical sensitivity by Middleton Murry
in chapter xv of his Shakespeare[30]—and finds, of course, no
satisfaction in the act. Curiously enough, what happens to Macbeth is closely similar to the effect of a different kind of lust on a
man's mind:

> Th' expense of spirit in a waste of shame
> Is lust in action; and till action, lust
> Is perjur'd, murd'rous, bloody, full of blame,
> Savage, extreme, rude, cruel, not to trust;
> Enjoy'd no sooner but despised straight;
> Past reason hunted, and, no sooner had,
> Past reason hated, as a swallowed bait,
> On purpose laid to make the taker mad—
> Mad in pursuit, and in possession so . . . etc.[31]

Shakespeare himself directs us to the rape of Lucrece (II. i. 55):
in his poem on this subject he had shown Tarquin with the same
reckless obsession before his crime, and the same disgust afterwards.

[27] I. vii. 1 et seq.   [28] I. v. 7, 8.   [29] I. vii. 27.
[30] First published in 1936.
[31] Sonnet 129. See my comment on this in Chapter 2.

Macbeth describes his own crime thus: 'Macbeth does murder sleep'.[32] In Holinshed's *Chronicles* there is an account of the murder of Malcolm Duff, which contains a passage on which Shakespeare probably drew for this speech. The murderer has concealed his crime, but cannot rest:

And (as the fame goeth) it chanced that a voice was heard as he was in bed in the night time to take his rest, vttering vnto him these or the like words in effect: 'Thinke not Kenneth that the wicked slaughter of Malcolm Duffe by thee contriued, is kept secret from the knowledge of the eternall God,' etc. . . . The king with this voice being striken into great dread and terror, passed that night without anie sleepe comming in his eies.[33]

In Macbeth's speech sleep and murder are combined into one powerful phrase: but it is clear from the source that Shakespeare had more than a merely literal sleeplessness in mind. Kenneth cannot sleep because of a conventional moral guilt; Macbeth is cut off from oblivion, the only escape from his horrible vision of himself. Middleton Murry describes it thus: '. . . He has murdered Sleep that is "the death of each day's life"—that daily death of Time which makes Time human. He has murdered that. Now he and his wife are become like the tortured criminal of China, whose eyelids are cut away: but this not in the physical, but the metaphysical realm. Time is now incessant . . .'[34]

After the crime, though the clock still shows the passing of time, the day is without light:

> . . . By th' clock 'tis day,
> And yet dark night strangles the travelling lamp.
> Is't night's predominance, or the day's shame
> That darkness does the face of earth entomb,
> When living light should kiss it?[35]

This murky world, where there are no distinctions between day and night,[36] where time is unpunctuated by its proper periods

---

[32] II. ii. 36.   [33] *Chronicles*, 1587, vol. 2, 'Historie of Scotland', p. 171.
[34] J. Middleton Murry, *Shakespeare*, 1965, p. 333.   [35] II. iv. 6 et seq.
[36] Mr. Nicholas Muska, of the University of California at Santa Barbara, has suggested to me an interesting symbolic reason for the weather of *Macbeth*: when the King, who is the 'sun' to his people, has been murdered, the sky is naturally dark. A similar symbolism operates in Richard II.

and changes, conveys an overwhelming feeling of oppressive-
ness, tedium, and unexcited horror. It is the world of Macbeth,
the world of 'incessant' time. Eliot's description of suburban
London has the same atmosphere:

> Here is a place of disaffection
> Time before and time after
> In a dim light: neither daylight
> Investing form with lucid stillness
> Turning shadow into transient beauty
> With slow rotation suggesting permanence
> Nor darkness to purify the soul
> Emptying the sensual with deprivation
> Cleansing affection from the temporal
> Neither plenitude nor vacancy. Only a flicker
> Over the strained time-ridden faces
> Distracted from distraction by distraction
> Filled with fancies and empty of meaning
> Tumid apathy with no concentration
> Men and bits of paper, whirled by the cold wind
> That blows before and after time,
> Wind in and out of unwholesome lungs
> Time before and time after.[37]

Indeed, Macbeth is not a small man, like Eliot's commuters; but
if we can make out an expression on his face, it is surely 'strained'
and 'time-ridden': his speech 'If it were done when 'tis done' and
his conversation with Lady Macbeth after the murder are 'Filled
with fancies and empty of meaning', 'Tumid apathy with no con-
centration'. Macbeth preserves our interest and sympathy only
because, like Milton's Satan, he carries with him a broken rem-
nant of his former greatness, which enables him to see what is
happening to himself. Dead souls are common: it is a rare and
terrible thing for a man to observe and be totally conscious of
his own spiritual death. Macbeth doesn't *want* to see himself,
and in the end he succeeds in blinding himself to himself; but by
that time he has seen and transmitted to us a unique vision of
moral horror.

[37] 'Burnt Norton', ll. 90 et seq.

Eliot's commuters are men who cannot bear facing the reality of the present moment, who live perpetually in the dead past or unborn future. Macbeth goes further: he commits a most horrible crime in the present, which cuts him off from the healing reality of 'now'; he does not only fear and avoid giving attention to the present, but actively defiles it. But both the commuters and Macbeth share a total boredom, a sense of hopeless tedium. The tomorrow for which Macbeth committed his crime will never come. This is the peculiar poetic justice of the play: if one places ones hopes in the future, one is placing one's joy in a time that will never be.

This, then, is the most obvious aspect of Macbeth's spiritual state after his crime—the accidie of a life which is cut off from the present moment. At the very beginning of the play we are given an image of Macbeth's predicament:

> ... And the very ports they blow,
> All the quarters that they know
> I' th' shipman's card.
> I'll drain him dry as hay:
> Sleep shall neither night nor day
> Hang upon his pent-house lid;
> He shall live a man forbid;
> Weary sev'nights, nine times nine,
> Shall he dwindle, peak, and pine.
> Though his bark cannot be lost,
> Yet it shall be tempest-tost.[38]

The Witches' torment of the shipman is subtle because it contains no final catastrophe, it has no 'end', either in the sense of purpose or of conclusion. Like Macbeth, the shipman is allowed no sleep, no punctuation of the process of time; nothing to divide today from tomorrow, to give new hope in a fresh start. The sea has often been a symbol of the huge rhythm of time which dominates our lesser human rhythms and from which there seems to be no escape; Eliot's fishermen find the same pointlessness in their voyages:

[38] I. iii. 15 et seq.

Where is the end of them, the fishermen sailing
Into the wind's tail, where the fog cowers?
We cannot think of a time that is oceanless
Or of an ocean not littered with wastage
Or of a future that is not liable
Like the past, to have no destination.[39]

Tedium is characterized by its lack of end, point, or 'destination'. Even mere physical sleep gives some direction to existence; but Macbeth cannot sleep, and for him there is only:

To-morrow, and to-morrow, and to-morrow,
Creeps in this petty pace from day to day
To the last syllable of recorded time,
And all our yesterdays have lighted fools
The way to dusty death. Out, out, brief candle!
Life's but a walking shadow, a poor player
That struts and frets his hour upon the stage,
And then is heard no more; it is a tale
Told by an idiot, full of sound and fury,
Signifying nothing.[40]

When we have stayed up all night, we often have the curious sensation that the next day is rather pointless, a mere continuation of the previous day. This is the basic physical referent of the image of sleeplessness; one usually finds when analysing Shakespeare's most powerful poetry, some common muscle-memory or physiological reflex at the bottom of it. This sleeplessness is the subjective equivalent of the gloomy weather and unpunctuated time of the play.

Life for Macbeth is not only tedious, it is also meaningless: a tale told by an idiot, signifying nothing. Words themselves lose their brightness and promise for him. The Witches greet Macbeth with the words 'All hail, Macbeth, that shalt be King hereafter!'[41] When Lady Macbeth greets him it is in almost religious terms: 'Greater than both, by the all-hail hereafter'[42]—words which might be used to describe a saint or prophet, but not a potential usurper. Finally, the word which once expressed not

[39] 'The Dry Salvages', ll. 67 et seq.   [40] V. v. 19 et seq.
[41] I. iii. 50.   [42] I. v. 52.

only his ambition, but also his faith in the supernatural powers of the Witches, becomes a bitter joke:

> She should have died hereafter;
> There would have been a time for such a word.[43]

Unless time is sanctified by the timeless, it can have no meaning: unless 'hereafter', future time, is validated by 'Hereafter', eternity, it is a tale told by an idiot.

The meaninglessness of the terms of Macbeth's existence is revealed to him, paradoxically, when he sees the words of the Witches coming true. When he hears that Birnam Wood has indeed come to Dunsinane, he admits that life no longer has any meaning for him:

> I gin to be aweary of the sun,
> And wish th' estate o' th' world were now undone.[44]

And when at last Macduff reveals the truth of the second prediction, Macbeth realizes how he has been deceived:

> And be these juggling fiends no more believ'd
> That palter with us in a double sense,
> That keep the word of promise to our ear,
> And break it to our hope![45]

Because Macbeth has been living on false meanings, his life has become meaningless.

The division between the literal meaning of the Witches' words and their apparent meaning, between Macbeth's outward innocence and inner guilt, and between the active self that can commit murder and the inner eye that must watch it happening, is expressed in the image of false clothing:

> . . . why do you dress me
> In borrowed robes?[46]

> New honours come upon him,
> Like our strange garments, cleave not to their mould
> But with the aid of use.[47]

Macbeth commits his crime for the sake of outward power, symbolized by the robes of state. As with the young man in the

[43] v. v. 17, 18.   [44] v. v. 49, 50.   [45] v. viii. 19 et seq.
[46] I. iii. 108 et seq.   [47] I. iii. 144 et seq.

sonnets such a dedication to temporal things brings about an inner corruption, masked by its outward show. His are 'borrowed robes'. Macbeth has become divided from his outer self, in an almost schizophrenic way. Further, he committed his crime on the basis of the apparent meaning of the Witches' predictions. Their real meaning, like the real meaning of Macbeth's life, is quite different from their outward seeming.

Another aspect of Macbeth's condition is the erosion of his freedom. Lady Macbeth claims that the murder of Duncan will

> . . . to all our nights and days to come
> Give solely sovereign sway and masterdom.[48]

There is an ironic ambiguity here: what Lady Macbeth means is that the murder will give them freedom and command over their existence: but the words literally mean that it will give sway and masterdom to their 'days and nights to come', in other words to the process of time in which they live. Macbeth thinks that the assassination might 'trammel up the consequence',[49] set him free in the course of action he has chosen. But at every turn Macbeth finds his margin of freedom diminishing. He must now kill Banquo; but the escape of Fleance destroys his hopes of getting the whole affair tied up and concluded:

> . . . I had else been perfect,
> Whole as the marble, founded as the rock,
> As broad and general as the casing air,
> But now I am cabin'd, cribb'd, confin'd, bound in
> To saucy doubts and fears.[50]

Macbeth committed his first murder for the sake of the freedom of action that power can give; he finds that instead of freedom, he gains only insecurity. As Macbeth equates security with freedom, he must commit another crime to protect both. His idea of freedom, which amounts to a merely temporal absence of restraint in a predictable future, can be usefully contrasted with the spiritual freedom of Lear at the end of the play: 'We two alone will sing like birds i' th' cage' etc.[51] But the freedom which

[48] I. v. 66, 67. [49] I. vii. 3.
[50] III. iv. 21 et seq. [51] *King Lear*, V. iii. 9.

knowing the future seems to offer is only illusory. If the future is known, it cannot be altered by free-will; the ignorance which living in the present seems to entail is part of our liberty. The 'ignorant present' that Lady Macbeth scorns, is our only claim to freedom.

From now on Macbeth's crimes follow with a remorseless logic, from which he himself cannot escape. If one decides to live entirely in relation to this 'bank and shoal of time', one must realize that one will be entirely governed by time's laws. By the end of the play Macbeth is totally controlled by his circumstances. In Act V scene v he still has the choice of remaining in the castle or making an attack on his enemies. By the end of the scene, 'There is nor flying hence nor tarrying here';[52] scene vii begins with the words:

> They have tied me to a stake; I cannot fly,
> But bear-like I must fight the course.[53]

One of the foundations of Macbeth's security, and consequently of his sense of freedom, has already proved baseless: the Birnam Wood prediction. Now the other is to be destroyed. When Macbeth meets Macduff on the field, and hears of his manner of birth, even his last choice, to fight on rather than commit suicide, is cut off: 'I'll not fight with thee',[54] says Macbeth, but now he must; there is no course of action left.

At the end of the play even Macbeth's senses seem to have been corrupted by the deadening weight of unremitting time. Like an old man, his way of life is fallen into the 'sere, the yellow leaf';[55] there is a dreary *Weltschmerz* in his reactions:

> I have almost forgot the taste of fears.
> The time has been my senses would have cool'd
> To hear a night-shriek, and my fell of hair
> Would at a dismal treatise rouse and stir
> As life were in't. I have supp'd full with horrors . . .[56]

Macbeth's senses, like an overloaded circuit, have gone dead. He receives the news of his wife's death with an almost casual bitterness.

---

[52] V. v. 48.   [53] V. vii. 1, 2.   [54] V. viii. 22.
[55] V. iii. 22.   [56] V. v. 9 et seq.

The reason for this curious apathy of perception can be approached in the 'dagger' scene:

> I have thee not, and yet I see thee still.
> Art thou not, fatal vision, sensible
> To feeling as to sight? or art thou but
> A dagger of the mind, a false creation,
> Proceeding from the heat-oppressed brain . . .
> Mine eyes are made the fools o' th' other senses,
> Or else worth all the rest.[57]

As Macbeth begins to spurn the present moment, and follow his imagination into a fancied future, his senses lose touch with reality—first the sense of sight ('What hands are here? Ha! They pluck out mine eyes'),[58] which is most firmly connected with the upper conscious regions of the mind, and at last the other senses, which would once have cooled 'to hear a night-shriek'. Having chosen the 'dagger of the mind' he will forever attempt to escape the healing touch of reality on his senses. Macbeth becomes oddly alienated from himself: 'The eye wink at the hand',[59] he says; he is trying to cut himself off from his own reality: a natural consequence of his cutting himself off from the present moment. Throughout the play the eye and the hand, the self and its actions in the real world, are opposed in Macbeth. The murder has made him a stranger to himself; we sense his appalling loneliness. He does not even have himself for company.

Macbeth always seems to be in a desperate hurry. We often observe in acquaintances who place great store by the future, a similar hurried preoccupation, a nervous inclination to forestall, as it were, their own compulsions and fears; to get ahead of events, almost as if they were running a race with time. We find this sense of nervous urgency in Macbeth's meditation on his intended crime:

> If it were done when 'tis done, the 'twere well
> It were done quickly . . .[60]

[57] II. i. 35 et seq.
[58] II. ii. 59. It may be helpful to keep in mind the 'I'–'eye' pun of the *Sonnets* at this point. Some of the ideas in this part of the chapter were suggested to me by Miss Toni Nanini, of the University of California at Santa Barbara.
[59] I. iv. 52.   [60] I. vii. 1, 2.

Ambition indeed 'o'erleaps itself'. Life for Macbeth is a 'fitful fever';[61] a literal fever can produce a feeling of hurry, as the heart beats faster and the temperature rises. He tries to get ahead of his own reflections:

> Strange things I have in head that will to hand,
> Which must be acted ere they may be scann'd.[62]

The verbal ellipsis 'in head', 'will to hand' heightens the feeling of urgency. Later he uses the image of a race to describe his relationship with time:

> Time, thou anticipat'st my dread exploits.
> The flighty purpose never is o'ertook
> Unless the deed go with it. From this moment
> The very firstlings of my heart shall be
> The firstlings of my hand. And even now,
> To crown my thoughts with acts, be it thought and
>   done . . .
> This deed I'll do before this purpose cool.[63]

Macbeth has the illusion that somehow, if he acts immediately enough on his impulses, he will be able to overtake the flow of time, that his inner 'eye' will be forestalled by his outer 'hand'. At the end of the play, when the army of his enemy is approaching, Macbeth's impatience becomes almost absurd. He screams at the 'cream-fac'd loon'[64] who brings him news; he puts on his armour before it is necessary; and he fights his last battle in an insane rush.

All this is a consequence of trying to live in the future. For a while Macbeth succeeds in retaining that power which such a course can give. There is a certain advantage in worldly affairs to be gained from a complete lack of scruple in present actions when they are aimed at a future goal; the man who has no regard for human and moral law has for a while the edge over his more conscientious acquaintances, whom he despises. Having made time future his special province, having limited and trained himself to such an element, he gains a temporary efficiency in a narrow sphere of action. But as with a modern revolutionary

[61] III. ii. 23.   [62] III. iv. 139, 140.
[63] IV. i. 144 et seq.   [64] V. iii. 11.

general, there comes a time when he must take account of that
which is timeless in Man; fighting a war is different from govern-
ing a country. The logistics of expediency no longer apply;
temporal efficiency is not enough. Those things in the universe
and in mankind which contradict the laws of time rise up to
destroy Macbeth. Birnam Wood indeed comes to Dunsinane:
what was thought physically impossible comes to pass. And
though Macbeth's specialization in the future makes him invulnerable to 'man of woman born', to ordinary, moral, law-abiding
humanity, he is at last vanquished by a man who

> ... was from his mother's womb
> Untimely ripp'd.[65]

Macbeth has not counted on this aspect of Man, the side of Man
that contradicts time, the 'untimely' powers of humanity. Macbeth's rejection of the supernatural in order to gain effectiveness
in the world of time makes him fatally vulnerable to the forces
of timelessness embodied in the victorious army of Malcolm.
'The time' is now 'free'.[66] From now on the 'grace of Grace' will
rule over actions performed in 'measure, time, and place'.[67]

[65] v. viii. 15, 16.   [66] v. viii. 55.   [67] v. viii. 72–3.

8. *The Speech of 'Time' in The Winter's Tale*[1]

THE speech of 'Time, the Chorus' at the beginning of Act IV of *The Winter's Tale* has divided its commentators as much, I imagine, as any Shakespearean crux.

Heath speaks of the 'insipid flatness' of the expression and writes the passage off as an 'interpolation of the players'. Capell traces the obscurity of the passage to the 'scarce discoverable' punctuation, but concludes that the passage is 'of the utmost use'. White declares that 'there can hardly be a greater difference in style than that between Time's speech as Chorus and the rest of this play. The former is direct, simple, composed of the commonest words used in their commonest signification, but bald and tame, and in its versification very constrained and ungraceful . . .' He speaks of its 'uncouth versification and enjambment'; and he too concludes that it was not written by Shakespeare. Lueders refers us to Greene's *Pandosto, or the Triumph of Time*, on the title-page of which appears the following: '. . . wherein is discovered . . . that, although by the meanes of sinister fortune, Truth may be concealed yet by Time in spight of fortune it is most manifestly revealed'. Stapfer assigns the passage a 'quiet and proud tone'; a 'dignified calmness and serenity'; while Hudson calls it 'clumsy, languid and obscure'.[2]

To dismiss a passage of Shakespeare as written by someone else has always been a favourite resource of critics and scholars who have either misunderstood its meaning or have been unable to fit it in with their own preconceptions of the dramatist's intention. We must approach this speech without trying to hide its seeming defects, and in an attempt to determine its true func-

[1] Since writing this chapter I have discovered I. S. Ewbank's article (in the *Review of English Literature*, 5, 1964), 'The Triumph of Time in the Winter's Tale'. Its methods and conclusions are largely different from mine.

[2] I have taken the above quotations of commentators from H. H. Furness's *New Variorum Edition* of *The Winter's Tale*, Philadelphia, 1898.

tion: Capell's remark about its being of the 'greatest use' should guide us here. We will find that an analysis of this speech will lead us to a wider consideration of the whole play, and perhaps a new vision of its totality.

Time's speech *is* obscure, as Hudson insists. We are, of course, familiar with the individual words, and there is no reason to assume that they are not used in their common 'significations'; but, as with 'beauty is truth', it is very difficult to get anything of significance out of these short, ambiguous phrases. We are accustomed to the rich vocabulary Shakespeare normally uses, filled with suggestion and connotation, pregnant with manifest meanings. The words in this speech are impenetrable: generalized and impassive, very different from the concrete and particular language Shakespeare seems to use even for his most universal philosophy.

Various points, however, should lead us to a realization of the importance of the speech of Time. First of all we note its dense and complex grammar, with the syntactical ambiguities which often appear when Shakespeare is bent on conveying difficult and important ideas. The second point is that the versification is very tough, displaying an 'asprezza' which forces the reader to a slow reading pace; filled with heavily accented long mono-syllables, yet, when it is read with the right weight and pace, very pleasant to the ear:

> . . . Impute it not a crime
> To me or my swift passage that I slide
> O'er sixteen years, and leave the growth untried
> Of that wide gap, since it is in my pow'r
> To o'erthrow law, and in one self-born hour
> To plant and o'erwhelm custom.[3]

The heavy rhymes, the large number of accented syllables per line, and the length and power of the syllables themselves (*crime, slide, o'er, years, leave, untried, wide, pow'r, o'erthrow, law, hour, o'erwhelm*) are used with an authority and gravity quite rare elsewhere in Shakespeare.

***

[3] IV. i. 4 et seq.

Moreover the contrast which White points out between the language of this speech and that of the rest of the play is itself a pointer to something of importance in it. The simplicity and impenetrability of the words are deliberate: we must think hard about them; they are receptacles for thought rather than thoughts themselves. When Dr. Johnson made his *Dictionary* he complained of the obduracy of these most basic words against definition; everybody understands them in his own way, and they can be used to define other words; but they themselves defy further analysis.[4] (We can define 'construct' by 'make'; it would be absurd to define 'make' by 'construct'.) Shakespeare's use of such language should alert us to the peculiar functions of this speech.

Time's speech comes at the pivot of the whole play, and must bring into relationship two extremes of Shakespeare's art. Here we have the widest range Shakespeare has ever attempted in one play, from black tragedy to bucolic comedy: from *Othello* to *As You Like It*. Something is happening in this speech which is at the core of Shakespeare's art. The simple, opaque words are a cable carrying the full strength of the play's thematic currents; the speech is at a high tension, as it were. In a similar fashion, the trite moral of *The Ancient Mariner*, 'he prayeth best who loveth best both man, and bird, and beast' carries the power of the whole poem's theme, and is made into a profound and valid statement about Man's nature by the terrible previous experiences of the Mariner. The speech of Time can likewise only be understood in the light of the rest of the play; and especially in the contrast and relationship of the first three acts with Act IV.

Time is deliberately rather enigmatic about himself. Shakespeare would have been quite capable of the copious and splendid time-poetry of the sonnets and of Lucrece's apostrophe at this point: but why attempt to say in a single speech what the whole play is saying far better? In *Pericles* where Shakespeare had similar ideas in mind, too much of the burden of the theme was borne by ancient Gower. Incidentally, Gower, with his white beard and coming from a distant past, must have seemed rather a similar figure to Father Time himself: and they play similar

---

[4] Samuel Johnson, *Dictionary of the English Language* (vol. i), 1824, pp. 5–6.

parts in their respective plays. In *The Winter's Tale*, however, it was enough to put Time on the stage, give him a speech of oracular obscurity, and let the play itself fill his words with particular meaning.

At this point I can clarify a source of difficulty in the text. Time says: 'I mention'd a son o' th' King's',[5] whereas he has not previously spoken of him in his one speech. However, I do not consider emendation to be necessary. Time says fairly explicitly that the story which follows is to be told by himself:

> ... but let Time's news
> Be known when 'tis brought forth. A shepherd's daughter
> And what to her adheres, which follows after,
> Is th' argument of Time.[6]

If Time is telling the *whole* story, from beginning to end, then he *did* mention a son of the king's. This idea is lent additional force by my suggestion of the parallel between Time and Gower, since Gower is very much the teller of *Pericles*. This parallel extends to a similarity in subject-matter and even to verbal similarities between Time and Gower, as may be seen in the following quotations from Gower's speeches:

> If you, born in those latter times,
> When wit's more ripe, accept my rhymes,
> And that to hear an old man sing
> I life would wish...[7]
> May to your wishes pleasure bring,

> ... The unborn event
> I do commend to your content;
> Only I carry winged time
> Post on the lame feet of my rhyme;
> Which never could I so convey
> Unless your thoughts went on my way.[8]

> Thus time we waste, and longest leagues make short;
> Sail seas in cockles, have an wish but for 't;
> Making, to take our imagination,
> From bourn to bourn, region to region.

[5] IV. i. 22.   [6] IV. ix. 26 et seq.
[7] *Pericles*, I, Prol. 11 et seq.   [8] Ibid., IV, Prol. 45 et seq.

> By you being pardon'd, we commit no crime
> To use one language in each several clime
> Where our scenes seem to live. I do beseech you
> To learn of me, who stand i' the' gaps to teach you
> The stages of our story.[9]

Time is like Gower: the teller of *The Winter's Tale*, and perhaps acted by Shakespeare himself on its first performances.

Time works a great change in this play:

> ... Your patience this allowing,
> I turn my glass, and give my scene such growing
> As you had slept between.[10]

This change is a highly complex one. As the teller of the tale, Time in a sense represents the dramatist himself; the glass is the hour-glass carried by Father Time, and the 'growing' is the growth of the tiny heap of sand, as well as an indication of the fruitful and creative effects of time. The image of sleep is also important: Shakespeare often uses it to convey the idea of healing; and it has the more mysterious connotations of dream, of the fantasy that is truth.

In the scene previous to that of Time's speech, the old shepherd had found a baby, whilst the clown had witnessed the destruction of the old world of the first three acts.

> ... thou met'st with things dying, I with things new-born.[11]

In every moment the old world dies and a new world is born. Time is for us a sequence of different moments, held together in an illusory way by the continuance of social institutions and outward appearances, but in the only real way by that which is timeless in us. In Time's speech 'one self-born hour'[12] perhaps implies that since the past is dead, every hour is self-generating; the present has a superficial resemblance to the immediate past, but that is all.

> Fare forward, you who think you are voyaging;
> You are not those who saw the harbour
> Receding, or those who will disembark.[13]

---

[9] Ibid., IV. iv. 1 et seq.   [10] IV. i. 15 et seq.   [11] III. iii. 109.
[12] IV. i. 8.   [13] T. S. Eliot, 'The Dry Salvages', ll. 149 et seq.

Time enters just after one of Shakespeare's severest 'sea-and-storm' scenes. G. Wilson Knight associates storm with tragedy, and the sea with that region of the human soul in which tragedy can occur.[14] This may very well be a useful idea; but there are other associations which are more interesting in this context. The sea in Shakespeare is frequently a symbol of the elemental processes of time:

> Like as the waves make towards the pebbled shore,
> So do our minutes hasten to their end;
> Each changing place with that which goes before,
> In sequent toil all forwards do contend.[15]

—and storms are often associated with change, as in *Pericles*. In *The Tempest* there was no need to incorporate the vast stretches of time that occur in *Pericles* and *The Winter's Tale*, because the effect of time on human personality had now been taken over by a symbol—that of the sea-change, a mixture of dream, drowning, and enchantment. In T. S. Eliot's poem, 'The Dry Salvages', the sea has a similar significance; and Time here as in that great poem is at once creator and destroyer:

> The river is within us, the sea is all about us;
> The sea is the land's edge also, the granite
> Into which it reaches, the beaches where it tosses
> Its hints of earlier and other creation:
> The starfish, the horseshoe crab, the whale's backbone;
> The pools where it offers to our curiosity
> The more delicate algae and the sea anemone.
> It tosses up our losses, the torn seine,
> The shattered lobsterpot, the broken oar
> And the gear of foreign dead men.[16]

S. L. Bethell finds in Shakespeare's treatment of the storm a kind of deliberate bathos.[17] Shakespeare comprehended in this scene both the good and the evil effects of change, so that there is a relativity of attitude as to what is happening. From the point of view of the old world the storm is tragic; but it is also the

---

[14] G. Wilson Knight, *The Shakespearian Tempest*, 1953.
[15] Sonnet 60.
[16] 'The Dry Salvages', ll. 15 et seq.
[17] S. L. Bethell, *The Winter's Tale, a Study*, 1947, p. 65.

beginning of the sweet comedy of the fourth act. Time himself shows a curious lightness in his comments on the story: but it is the lightness of one who is above the folly of man. *Sub specie aeternitatis* human affairs lose their obsessive importance: Leontes's mad tyranny is after all only 'fond jealousies':[18]

> ... and make stale
> The glistering of this present, as my tale
> Now seems to it.[19]

The imagery of the storm itself is instructive here:

> ... now the ship boring the moon with her mainmast, and anon swallowed with yeast and froth, as you'd thrust a cork into a hogshead ... to see how the sea flap-dragon'd it ... .[20]

The storm is like the fermentation of a barrel of beer: the decay of one thing but the brewing up of something better. In *The Tempest* the 'black cloud' is a 'bombard that would shed his liquor'.[21] Perhaps there is even a suggestion of the effects of strong drink: forgetfulness, loss of care, sleep; and indeed these scenes are not only a transition in the play; they also give us an almost dreamlike detachment, so that we may see the two halves of the play in proper perspective.

Time's speech, then, is of profound importance spatially, as the connection between the two halves of *The Winter's Tale*, and as part of the great transformation which includes the storm scene. But Time's speech not only conducts us across the widest gap of mood and of imagined time in Shakespeare, it also plumbs the very nature of time; the change is not a mere scene-change, but Change itself. Shakespeare would, one is sure, have had no difficulty in telescoping his story if he wanted to avoid this large and perhaps inartistic hiatus: but the gap of sixteen years, the change of mood, *dramatis personae,* locale, and manner are all deliberate. Drama's essentials are action and change; Shakespeare is here consciously comprehending as huge a change as possible, and is approaching, perhaps, the very mainspring that makes drama work. Human change is here accelerated, so that

[18] IV. i. 18.   [19] IV. i. 13 et seq.
[20] III. iii. 90–5.   [21] *The Tempest*, II. ii. 20.

we may see it organically, like a speeded-up film of a flower opening.

But 'Time, the Chorus' does not stand only for that aspect of time that we call change. Time is, perhaps, the most fundamental feature of Man's environment. In Shakespeare's plays the unhappy and evil characters are those who are out of harmony with their environment; in *The Winter's Tale* this environment is the domain of Time. Before Time's speech the individual and society do not stand in a proper relation to time: after it, the true relationship is restored. Leontes misunderstands and misuses time, so that the world beyond time (represented by the oracle) must be invoked to redress the balance; and the destructive forces of time must test and assay what was of value in the first three acts:

> I, that please some, try all, both joy and terror
> Of good and bad . . .[22]

Time is both hero and villain of *The Winter's Tale*: Man's obsession with time brings about his downfall, but the laws of time itself can help effect a cure.

In order fully to understand the importance of Time's speech we must, therefore, examine Man's relationship with his temporal environment in both the tragic and the pastoral phases of *The Winter's Tale*. Before the fourth act both the individual and society are sick; and the healing that follows is both a social and an individual one. I shall deal first with time and the individual, then with time and society.

Time pleases some, but tries all, the joy and terror of good and evil men. To 'try' something is to refine away and reject that which cannot endure in it. If Man is wholly a temporal being, then he is wholly subject to the laws of time—of decay and fate: when time tries him, he will be found wanting in that which endures, that which is independent of time.

Throughout the first three acts there is an oppressive and unremitting sense of time as the master of human affairs, rather than as Man's servant:

[22] IV. i. 1, 2.

> Nine changes of the wat'ry star hath been
> The shepherd's note since we have left our throne
> Without a burden . . .[23]

> One sev'night longer.[24]

> I love thee not a jar o' th' clock behind
> What lady she her lord.[25]

> Three crabbed months had sour'd themselves to death,
> Ere I could make thee open thy white hand.[26]

> . . . Wishing clocks more swift;
> Hours, minutes; noon, midnight?[27]

> . . . she would not live
> The running of one glass.[28]

Over the whole of this part of the play there broods the impression of a sweet and innocent past which has gone forever, stolen away by time. This aspect of time is similar to that of the Sonnets, where it becomes the destroyer of beauty, youth, and even love, if we permit it. Opposed to this vision is that of the boys Mamillius and Florizel who can work those small miracles with time that are the prerogatives of the pure in heart. Mamillius 'makes old hearts fresh';[29] Florizel 'makes a July's day short as December.'[30] Leontes and Polixenes, too, once possessed this quality of timelessness:

> Two lads that thought there was no more behind
> But such a day to-morrow as to-day
> And to be boy eternal.[31]

But this innocence has passed away; and the faith that could keep it alive is dead. Faith, indeed, is one of the few human attributes that can resist the destructive testing of time. It is in faith that people get married, a blind act of belief that what is loved will remain despite the ravages of change. Shakespeare describes this in Sonnet 116; and the greatest agony suffered by any Shakespearean character is the destruction of the faith in that which is timeless in Man: Lear's faith in his daughters' love,

[23] I. ii. 1 et seq.   [24] I. ii. 17.   [25] I. ii. 43, 44.
[26] I. ii. 102, 103.   [27] I. ii. 289, 290.   [28] I. ii. 305, 306.
[29] I. i. 36.   [30] I. ii. 169.   [31] I. ii. 63 et seq.

Hamlet's faith in his mother's purity, and Pericles' faith in Antiochus' daughter; Othello is faced by the dilemma that you cannot prove what you must most deeply believe, for proof and faith are of different worlds.

Leontes' jealousy is a similar loss of faith. Images of winter, old age, prison, and blindness symbolize this death of the spirit. The rational world, the world of proof, has trespassed on regions where it is destructive. Jealousy forgets the inner spirit, and dwells on minute external physical details: 'paddling palms' and 'pinching fingers';[32] 'leaning cheek to cheek', 'meeting noses', 'Kissing with inside lip', 'horsing foot on foot'.[33] A person is not a collection of details which we can add up like an 'identikit' picture, but a 'thou'.

This is the first stage of the rational process of proof: the accumulation of facts. Now Leontes enters the second stage, *deduction* from these facts as to Hermione's mental state, and *comparison* of these facts with the generalized and conventional picture of unfaithfulness:

> . . . Many thousand on's
> Have the disease, and feel't not.[34]

To compare is to reduce what is compared to the level of what it is compared with: but in matters of love comparison must be irrelevant; we must love a person for his own sake only. If love is comparable, then it is not sublime, not peerless to itself. And if it is not these, then it is not love. (Lear committed this error when he attempted to compare the love of his daughters.)

The 'intellect that kills' has had its deadly effect. Leontes is almost proud of what he considers his superior consciousness, in an ironic way:

> . . . Not noted, is't,
> But of the finer natures, by some severals
> Of head-piece extraordinary?[35]

(It is interesting to note how Shakespeare uses the extravagant language of the 'wit' here.) Leontes has become bound up in the world of reasons and causes. He assumes that Hermione is acting

[32] I. ii 115.   [33] I. ii. 285.
[34] I. ii. 206, 207.   [35] I. ii. 225 et seq.

compulsively, driven by external physical and social forces, and
the assumption causes him to act just as compulsively himself:

> Swear his thought over
> By each particular star in heaven and
> By all their influences, you may as well
> Forbid the sea for to obey the moon
> As or by oath remove or counsel shake
> The fabric of his folly . . .[36]

Leontes has allowed his faith to be changed; and has plunged
himself into a deterministic pattern, governed by the compulsions of his own false logic. As a result, the very springs of perception itself are tainted:

> Alack, for lesser knowledge! How accurs'd
> In being so blest! There may be in the cup
> A spider steep'd, and one may drink, depart,
> And yet partake no venom, for his knowledge
> Is not infected; but if one present
> Th' abhorred ingredient to his eye, make known
> How he hath drunk, he cracks his gorge, his sides
> With violent hefts. I have drunk, and seen the spider.[37]

It is only a proper use of time that can cure this 'infected knowledge': Leontes must suffer sixteen years' penance before Hermione is restored to him. And he must believe the impossible,
and forget the outward seeming, when the statue comes to life.

After Time's speech we are given a vision of Man in harmony
with his temporal environment: and this harmony consists in a
reconciliation of time and the timeless. As Bethell points out,
'Time is himself timeless, outside the changing process of
history.'[38]

> . . . Let me pass
> The same I am, ere ancient'st order was
> Or what is now receiv'd. I witness to
> The times that brought them in; so shall I do
> To th' freshest things now reigning, and make stale
> The glistering of this present, as my tale
> Now seems to it.[39]

[36] I. ii. 424 et seq.   [37] II. i. 38 et seq.
[38] Op. cit., p. 39.   [39] IV. i. 9 et seq.

Like T. S. Eliot's 'timeless moment', the flower-passage in Act IV scene iv has a breathless and instantaneous quality, as when we feel that the present moment is very close to eternity.

> ... daffodils
> That come before the swallow dares, and take
> The winds of March with beauty; violets, dim
> But sweeter than the lids of Juno's eyes
> Or Cytherea's breath ...[40]

Here beauty, 'whose action is no stronger than a flower',[41] for all its fragility, is somehow beyond the killing touch of time. Perdita moves in a dance which is 'still, and still moving' in this passage:

> ... When you do dance, I wish you
> A wave o' th' sea, that you might ever do
> Nothing but that; move still, still so,
> And own no other function ...

(Here the sea-image is used once more, but in a different way: a wave moves, while the water itself is still. Perdita's beauty is the reconciliation of time and eternity: of movement and stillness.)

> ... Each your doing,
> So singular in each particular,
> Crowns what you are doing in the present deeds,
> That all your acts are queens.[42]

This sense of peerlessness, the superlatives and hyperbole, contrast sharply with Leontes' obsessive comparisons and generalizations earlier in the play.

The reconciliation of the temporal and eternal worlds is symbolized in Act IV by the image of gods incarnate in animal form; indeed, Perdita and Florizel are Princess and Prince in the guise of shepherds:

> ... The gods themselves,
> Humbling their deities to love, have taken
> The shapes of beasts upon them: Jupiter

---

[40] IV. iv. 118 et seq.   [41] Sonnet 65.   [42] IV iv. 140 et seq.

> Became a bull and bellow'd; the green Neptune
> A ram and bleated; and the fire-rob'd god,
> Golden Apollo, a poor humble swain,
> As I seem now.[43]

The animal imagery reinforces the impression we have of the young lovers, of that innocence and consistency that animals possess. When human beings are truly innocent, without sin to fragment their natures or jealousy to divide man from man, they share this blessed wholeness. Leontes had allowed his rational faculty to divide him, so that one half of his mind kept watch on the other. Perdita and Florizel are singleminded, determined not by external forces but by their inner spirit.

> *Flo*: What, like a corse?
> *Per*: No; like a bank for love to lie and play on;
>   Not like a corse; or if—not to be buried,
>   But quick, and in mine arms.[44]

The little phrases, each broken off, have the spontaneity of a child's; she is speaking as she feels. Perdita is a person, not a self-imposed type like the jealous Leontes. Florizel, unlike Leontes, will not give up his faith:

> It cannot fail but by
> The violation of my faith; and then
> Let nature crush the sides o' th' earth together
> And mar the seeds within![45]

Florizel identifies faith with the essential fertility of the earth, of which his own sexual love is a part. His faith is not tainted by causes and reasons, and hence it can endure the testing of change. In the Sonnets one of the defences of love against Time was procreation; in this part of *The Winter's Tale* fertility and generation have a spiritual value.

The will is now free of time, and consequently of the fixed and ingrown attitudes that can pervert it; it can act in a sweet harmony with all the other faculties of Man. This faith is deeply founded: not for all that the 'earth wombs' or the 'seas hides'[46]

---

[43] IV. iv. 25 et seq.   [44] IV. iv. 129 et seq.
[45] IV. iv. 468 et seq.   [46] IV. iv. 482.

will Florizel break his faith: and these are the regions of ultimate power, to which Prospero returns his book and staff.

It is not only the individual's relationship with his temporal environment, but also society's, which is sick and is cured in *The Winter's Tale*. Time acts as the destroyer of the structure of society:

> ... it is in my pow'r
> To o'erthrow law, and in one self-born hour
> To plant and o'erwhelm custom.[47]

This overthrow of law and custom, and the ensuing scenes in which social distinctions disappear and social conventions are flouted, are necessary because, as in *As You Like It*, society had become a prison. The tyranny of Leontes and the tyranny of temporal and deterministic fate hang over it: 'There's some ill planet reigns'.[48] For Leontes' rule has become a tyranny, which instead of protecting the freedom of his subjects, destroys it. And there are more fundamental ills:

> Fear you his tyrannous passion more, alas,
> Than the Queen's life?[49]

There are two powers in society, it seems: the power of the strong and the power of the weak. The power of the strong, of wealth, force, birth, and legal rights, is what preserves political and social institutions, which in turn give continuity, stability, and security to men, and protect them against change. Social institutions at their best are a way of minimizing the malign effects of time; at their worst, they impose a temporal tyranny on us.

But there is another and opposite hierarchy of power—the power of sacred weakness. The very old and the very young, the ailing, even the insane,[50] command of us imperatively respect and generosity. If we entertain a beggar he may be Jove, or Christ; chivalry to women is founded on our respect for sacred weakness. This power is that of the Kingdom of Ends,[51] not the

---

[47] IV. i. 7 et seq.   [48] II. i. 105.   [49] II. iii. 28, 29.

[50] And also fools: see my remarks on Feste in Chapter IV.

[51] For an interesting critical use of this phrase see Arthur Sewell, *Character and Society in Shakespeare*, 1951, pp. 30–3, and also Chap. V of that book. It was first used by Immanuel Kant.

Kingdom of Means: when we obey it we are recognizing the ultimate value of human life, the inalienable rights of basic humanity. Here this power is represented by the boy Mamillius, the baby Perdita, and the 'Queen's life'. Camillo and Antigonus are forced to choose between the two powers: both choose that of the Kingdom of Ends, the power of sacred weakness.

But Leontes' court is a tyranny: the powers of the weak have been crushed; there is only one power, the power of the strong, in this society. All the characters are locked in a system where the only authority is the King's. The social institution of kingship has become rigid, a prison insusceptible to the healing influences that come from beyond time. Society has lost its inner spirit, like the society that Lear arraigns in his madness; and before the statue can come back to life, Time must work his great change.

Time's speech overthrows the laws and customs of society, that it may be healed. And so follows a 'self-born hour', a period far away from the time of the first three acts and divided by a journey from the last act; in a society the very opposite of that of Leontes, and where indeed the thief Autolycus is tolerated, and a prince can marry a shepherdess. I should like to borrow a term from Social Anthropology and characterize this act as a 'liminal' period, on the threshold between one state of society and another, not bound by the ordinary laws of time and society. Bethell's amusing idea that the 'seacoast of Bohemia' is a deliberate impossibility[52] seems to be on the right track: it is from Never-Never Land or Oz that society is rejuvenated. The world of romance, of *A Midsummer Night's Dream*, the 'golden world' of *As You Like It,* Illyria, and Belmont, have the same quality.[53]

In this part of the play the powers of the weak are in the ascendant. False distinctions disappear, the distinctions which preserve the powers of the strong when they turn to tyranny. Prince and Princess are equal to the shepherds: they are equal in their common humanity, in the *comitatus* of flesh and blood and the shared essentials of sunshine and ale:

[52] Op. cit., pp. 32–5.
[53] Cf., 'escapism' in Chapter 4.

For a quart of ale is a dish for a King.[54]
The self-same sun that shines upon his court
Hides not his visage from our cottage, but
Looks on alike.[55]

Here the tyranny of the first three Acts is abolished, and a cure can begin.

We have followed the clues offered to us in the style of Time's speech, in its immediate context of the great change, and in its wider context of the whole play. In *The Winter's Tale*, where the dramatist is more than usually visible behind the scenes, guiding and controlling the plot, and even in a sense telling the story, it is surely significant that a speech of such structural and thematic importance should be put into the mouth of Time. 'Time as Chorus' is not merely a sort of stage-manager smoothing over Shakespeare's violation of the Three Unities; he expresses and represents the basic mystery of *The Winter's Tale*: the strange, ambiguous nature of change and of Man's environment, the world of time.

[54] IV. iii. 8.
[55] IV. iv. 436 et seq.

9. Conclusion: the Living Statue

The light of the body is the eye: if therefore thine eye be single,
thy whole body shall be full of light. But if thine eye be evil,
thy whole body shall be full of darkness. If therefore the light
that is in thee be darkness, how great is that darkness!
                                      Matthew 6: 22 (Authorized Version)

AT the end of *The Winter's Tale* Shakespeare brings off a
dramatic audacity which sums up many of the themes with which
I have dealt in this study.

In the play Perdita and Florizel have been re-united with the
world by which they were rejected. In them an intense spirituality
and sense of the timeless is reconciled with that feeling of the
warm and living touch of reality so characteristic of Shakespeare's
idealism—and this spirit is breathed into the world of deterministic logic, tyrannous passion, of empty social forms and
imprisoning time, which we were shown in the first three Acts.
They bring this world to life again, and the effect is, oddly
enough, like a statue coming to life.[1] The image would be per-
fectly appropriate, and Shakespeare might well have embodied
it in some lines of poetry. Instead, he now presents it as a fact on
the stage, with a daring that is scarcely matched elsewhere in
literature or drama. The effect is doubly powerful: on the poetic
level, an image literally becomes reality; on the dramatic level,
a statue becomes a woman. This is closer to sacrament than to
symbol, though theological explanations would be impertinent.

We have seen how in the sonnets time is the great destroyer.
In this last scene of *The Winter's Tale* a death seems to have been
repealed; 'all losses' are here 'restor'd, and sorrows end'.[2] Time
the destroyer has somehow been thwarted.

Time's assault is specifically against the externals of persons

---

[1] The conversation between the two gentlemen about the return of Perdita is a
rhetorical example of this. Beneath the conceits and the elegance is a tremendous
life and power that vitalizes them. The conceited verbalism of the court is given
a subject that brings it alive.   [2] Sonnet 30.

and things, and an obsession with external could, in the sonnets and in *Twelfth Night* and *Macbeth*, destroy the inner spirit. Leontes had placed his credence in the externals of unfaithfulness, but ignored the true heart of his wife, rather as Malvolio placed his trust in cross-garters and lost any sensitivity to the emotional facts of his situation; or as Macbeth sought the outward trappings of power but found that they did not imply an inner happiness. This problem is important also in *Love's Labour's Lost*, *Richard II*, and *King Lear*; and there is a closer analogue in *Othello*, where the Moor puts his trust not in his wife but in external evidence of unfaithfulness. But in this scene the inner spirit seems to be breathed back into the shell of a statue's appearance and into Leontes' purged heart. He finds

> ... the first conceit of love there bred,
> Where time and outward form would show it dead.[3]

When Leontes wonders 'Still, methinks, There is an air comes from her. What fine chisel Could ever yet cut breath?',[4] we sense that here is a final answer to the terrible problems raised by Lear's

> ... Lend me a looking-glass;
> If that her breath will mist or stain the stone,
> Why, then she lives.[5]

Among other things the statue-Hermione is a test. There are many tests in *The Winter's Tale*: time itself is one.[6] The 'statue' is the final trial of Leontes' long penance, and it tests those powers of perception that Leontes had abused. The 'statue' is a tremendous paradox of appearance and reality. It seems to be a statue, but it is not what it seems; but its outward appearance is Hermione, and it is indeed what it seems.

In the sonnets we saw how Shakespeare was obsessed with the problem of perception and reality. There were, it seemed, at least two types of subjective perception; the perception of lust was less honest than the ordinary evidence of the senses; the perception of love and faith was able to ignore the merely superficial

---

[3] Sonnet 108.
[5] *King Lear*, v. iii. 261 et seq.
[4] v. iii. 77, 78.
[6] See Chapter 8.

aspects of sense and penetrate to the reality beneath. A surrender to sense destroyed sense: there was a certain type of sense perception that did not connect a man with reality, but cut him off from it. In *Twelfth Night* Malvolio's appetite was distempered, and, though his senses were more than usually active, his lust and desire for power came between him and reality. In *Hamlet* Gertrude's 'apoplex'd' sense chose the satyr rather than Hyperion. Macbeth's crime weakened the powers of his senses to restore that contact with reality that could cure him. In *Othello* the Moor's hold on reality was loosened when his vision began to edit what he saw in accord with his jealous obsession; the perception of jealousy is not essentially different from the perception of lust. Leontes seized on precisely the same details of countenance and behaviour as do the febrile senses of the lecher, but his reaction was not one of voluptuousness but of disgust.

In the first three Acts of *The Winter's Tale* Leontes had been using the lust- or jealousy-type of perception; when he insists that the 'statue' is Hermione herself he is using the love- or faith-type of perception. The paradox of the 'statue' is a precise assay of these types of sense. Leontes must repudiate the one in insisting that the 'statue' is not a statue; and he must cleave with all his being to the other in order to believe that the 'statue' is truly Hermione. We have been able to see this kind of relativity in perception throughout the plays and poetry; but here the distinction is clearest and the problem stated in its most elegant form. What are the basic differences between 'true sight'[7] and the apparently brilliant vision of spiritual blindness?

Leontes says of the 'statue':

> ... Does not the stone rebuke me
> For being more stone than it?[8]

The rebuke is twofold. Leontes had indeed been stone in his treatment of his wife: devoid of human feeling, smothering the subjective sanity of his own personal knowledge of his wife in a fury of objective analysis. But there is more to this remark: the

---

[7] Sonnet 148.   [8] v. iii. 37, 38.

point is that Leontes had treated his wife as if she were stone, as if she were inanimate, subject to the mechanics of objects and meriting no human insight. Leontes had seen his wife as operating like a machine according to the deterministic laws that rule over non-human things. Whilst Leontes was treating his wife as stone, as unhuman, he himself had been more stone that she. There is a delicate irony in the fact that in order for the stone to come to life, Leontes must believe that it is alive and human: whereas before he had believed his living wife to be as stone. Thus the first distinction we can make between false and true sight is that where human beings are concerned, false sight petrifies or makes into an object that which it perceives, like a Gorgon's head: true sight brings what seems inanimate to life. It gilds 'the object whereupon it gazeth'.[9] False sight, like Tarquin's lustful vision in *Lucrece*, kills like a 'cockatrice's eye'.[10] There is an exquisite image of this towards the end of *Othello*, where the Moor's jealous vision has turned his wife to stone or ice:

... Yet I'll not shed her blood,
Nor scar that whiter skin of hers than snow,
And smooth as monumental alabaster.[11]

Paulina prepares to wake the 'statue'. She tells Leontes:

... It is requir'd
You do awake your faith.[12]

The theme of faith has been important in the ideas we have explored in this study. It is faithful love that is Shakespeare's final refuge in the sonnets:

... Love is not love
Which alters when it alteration finds,
Or bends with the remover to remove.
O, no! it is an ever-fixed mark,
That looks on tempests and is never shaken;
It is the star to every wand'ring bark,
Whose worth's unknown, although his height be
taken.[13]

[9] Sonnet 20.
[10] *The Rape of Lucrece*, l. 540.
[11] *Othello*, v. ii. 3 et seq.
[12] v. iii. 94, 95.
[13] Sonnet 116.

The immutability of human faith is here expressed in the image of the North Star, which does not move in the sky; and this is an image of the incomparability of true love. Measurement is irrelevant to it: it exists in the sphere of values, in a world where comparison is odious. Cleopatra's teasing 'I'll set a bourn how far to be belov'd' is answered by Antony in great words: 'Then must thou needs find out new heaven, new earth.'[14] Hamlet is appalled by the attitude of his mother to his father's death: it seems to him that she has measured off precisely how much she loved her husband in the length of her mourning: '. . . die two months ago, and not forgotten yet?'[15] True love 'alone stands hugely politic, That it nor grows with heat nor drowns with show'rs',[16] it is not tainted with reasons and comparisons. But it was reasons and comparisons that destroyed Leontes' love in the first three acts of *The Winter's Tale*, and produced his spiritual blindness. Keats complained of Coleridge's 'irritable reaching after fact and reason'; we, and Leontes, must be 'content with half-knowledge' that the 'statue' may come to life. Macbeth's attempt to turn the half-knowledge of the witches' prophecy into the full knowledge of fact resulted in an appalling breach of faith, and in the blindness to his fate and the delusions of security to which he succumbs.

Camillo's remark, in which he compares the making of the 'statue' with the penance of Leontes:

> . . . Scarce any joy
> Did ever so long live; no sorrow
> But kill'd itself much sooner.[17]

answers the bitter cynicism of the Player King in *Hamlet*:

> Most necessary 'tis that we forget
> To pay ourselves what to ourselves is debt.
> What to ourselves in passion we propose,
> The passion ending, doth the purpose lose.
> The violence of either grief or joy
> Their own enactures with themselves destroy.[18]

---

[14] *Antony and Cleopatra*, I. i. 16, 17.   [15] *Hamlet*, III. ii. 125.
[16] Sonnet 124.   [17] V. iii. 51 et seq.   [18] *Hamlet*, III. ii. 187 et seq.

The true sight which can give life is the vision of faith. This is a second criterion of true and false sight: in human relationships, true sight is the insight of faith; false sight is the intrusion of the reason, the 'intellect that kills' into areas where it does not belong.

Leontes' attitude to the 'statue' has a curious passivity or receptiveness about it. Everything in the room seems stilled:

> ... What you can make her do
> I am content to look on; what to speak
> I am content to hear ...[19]

> ... Proceed.
> No foot shall stir.[20]

This is in contrast with the fervid reasoning, the adduction of causes and the deduction from observation by which perception is accompanied in Leontes' mind in the first three Acts. Everything he observed was placed in a deterministic sequence of cause and effect. Leontes was at once determined by the stimuli of what he saw, and at the same time convinced that what he saw was part of a logical process, a deterministic pattern of unfaithfulness. When we see others as acting deterministically, then we may have begun to be deterministic ourselves. We remember Malvolio, for instance, obsessed with the idea that his mistress is in love with him, seeing every action or word of hers as determined by that love, when he himself was locked to the rails of a sequence of motive, stimulus, and cause. Hamlet, looking at the army of Fortinbras, envied the young soldier in that he seemed to have freed himself from cause and effect in his absurd war; Hamlet himself is caught in the deterministic chain of his own reasoning. In order to act or suffer he must have a valid cause for action or suffering: but the moment he asks for a cause he has ceased to act and he and his senses are poisoned. It is only when Hamlet can free himself from cause that he is able to see clearly where is his duty and what he must do. Hamlet's 'the readiness is all'[21] is parallel to Leontes' 'I am content to look on'. Macbeth, caught in a political sequence of

---

[19] v. iii. 91 et seq.   [20] v. iii. 97, 98.   [21] *Hamlet*, v. ii. 214.

cause and effect, finds the freshness of his senses dulled: what he *must* do and *must* feel cannot be done or felt of his own accord: consequently the self is alienated from the world in which it feels and acts.

The true perception that unites, rather than alienates, has a certain impartiality. Whatever Hamlet is to see or do, he is ready. Leontes is 'content', never mind what the 'statue' will do in his presence. And when the vision has appeared, there is no attempt to fit it in with causes or predict effects: there is only wonder:

> This is the air; that is the glorious sun;
> This pearl she gave me, I do feel't and see't;
> And though 'tis wonder that enwraps me thus,
> Yet 'tis not madness.[22]

> ... O, wonder!
> How many goodly creatures are there here!
> How beauteous mankind is! O brave new world
> That has such people in't![23]

True sight accepts completely what it sees, on its own merits, without any attempt to make causal chains or logical sequences out of what one sees. Any connections of this kind must be implicit in what one sees: one must not impose one's own patterns on that which has its own. The true sight of love was expressed in the Sonnets in almost existentialist terms:

> In him those holy antique hours are seen,
> Without all ornament, itself and true ...[24]

Thus we have another basis of distinction between false and true sight: false sight sees a thing as part of a causal chain, or a person as merely a number of deterministic motives; true sight sees the *Ding an sich*: it is pure receptivity in perception, and pure wonder in comprehension.

The 'statue' is woken:

> *Paul*: ... Then all stand still;
> Or those that think it is unlawful business
> I am about, let them depart.

[22] *Twelfth Night*,)ff. iii 1. et seq.   [23] *The Tempest*, v. i. 181 et seq.
[24] Sonnet 68.

Leon: Proceed.
No foot shall stir.
Paul: Music, awake her: strike. [*Music.*
'Tis time; descend; be stone no more; approach;
Strike all that look upon with marvel. Come;
I'll fill your grave up. Stir; nay, come away.
Bequeath to death your numbness, for from him
Dear life redeems you. You perceive she stirs.
[*Hermione comes down from the pedestal.*
Start not; her actions shall be holy as
You hear my spell is lawful. Do not shun her
Until you see her die again; for then
You kill her double. Nay, present your hand.
When she was young you woo'd her; now in age
Is she become the suitor?
Leon: O, she's warm!
If this be magic, let it be an art
Lawful as eating.[25]

There is a hushed, reverent tone about the first half of this passage, and in Leontes' reaction to the movement of the 'statue'. The words are almost whispered: there are few strong vowels but many lingering sibilants and consonant clusters. An 'asprezza' or harshness compels the actor to speak slowly and hesitantly, suggesting that the speaker is venturing with temerity where angels fear to tread: Paulina is a high priestess whose commands and invocations are directed at forces that she is not worthy, except as priestess, to command or invoke. Leontes is in the state of complete receptivity and awe that is associated with religious experience. In the short, breathless phrases of the awakening of the 'statue', time seems to stand still:

'Tis time; descend; be stone no more; approach.

As the 'statue' begins to move and show human characteristics the language relaxes into a controlled triumph: 'dear life redeems you'; and finally a smile appears on Paulina's face as she gently mocks Leontes' immobility.

But for a moment we have seen time and the timeless intersect. The first step of Hermione does not seem to be within the

[25] v. iii. 95 et seq.

dispensation of time. There is a sense of stillness (indeed, the word 'still' is used by Paulina): an immobility that is not strained, and a feeling of eternity or permanence (the other meaning of 'still'); which are not irreconcilable with movement, power, and even energy. The 'statue' moving is like T. S. Eliot's 'still point of the turning wheel': because time has no jurisdiction over it, there is no contradiction between movement and stillness. We have seen this effect before, when Florizel wishes Perdita were a wave of the sea, that she might 'ever do Nothing but that; move still, still so, And own no other function'.[26]

In *Hamlet* the timeless world erupted into the world of time with the appearance of the Ghost. But there the timeless was outside law, it was terrifying, dark, and there was a certain ambiguity as to whether it was evil or good that had broken into the world of men. The Ghost's appearance was contrasted with the Nativity of Christ and compared with the dead breaking unnaturally from their graves. The timeless is as yet menacing and unfriendly. In *Macbeth* timeless forces acted against the usurper, so that where Macbeth is willing to violate the natural law of time there is an unnatural, timeless law that can overthrow him. The timeless in *Macbeth* is an avenging angel without much benevolence to humanity.

But in this last scene of *The Winter's Tale* Leontes touches his wife and exclaims 'O, she's warm!'. The timeless has become something friendly, even familiar. Paulina tells Leontes to woo his wife. The human and the divine worlds are reconciled:

> If this be magic, let it be an art
> Lawful as eating.

The timeless is no longer outside human law:

> ... those that think it is unlawful business
> I am about, let them depart.

> ... her actions shall be holy as
> You hear my spell is lawful.

The true sight which Leontes has gained is perhaps the capacity to see that which is timeless in the flux of time; based on a

[26] IV. iv. 141–3.

moral vision which is itself uncorrupted by those aspects of time that can destroy the inner spirit. In human relationships, to see the person rather than the thing is to see something which is not entirely of the temporal world, something not completely limited by the confines of time. A person can grow, and contradict the law of time that rules that all things must decay; and the actions of a person cannot be explained only by the temporal laws of cause and effect. Again, to see human beings not only with the eye of reason, but also with the eye of faith, is to use a faculty which is in some respects beyond the touch of time. Reason is based on temporal relations which become a logic; faith is closer to the inner self of a man, so that we can say that what a man reasons, he knows; but what a man believes, he is. Faith can endure blows that would shatter a concept based merely on reason. And faith is the only ultimate basis of human relationships. The third distinction between true and false sight that we saw in the test of Leontes was the difference between seeing a thing as a link in a causal chain, and seeing it as itself. Shakespeare had complained that 'what we see doth lie, Made more or less, by [time's] continual haste';[27] false vision, perhaps, sees the falsifications of time, but true vision can penetrate them. That Leontes' vision, moreover, is neither cold nor ethereal, does not show that it is not spiritual or, in its own way, timeless; rather it should point out to us just what Shakespeare saw as timeless and spiritual. Shakespeare was no Albigensian, and often his greatest spiritual and eternal values are found expressed and immanent in intense physical or emotional feelings. Consider the dying Cleopatra, to whom death is a lover's pinch or a baby at the breast; or the spirituality we feel in the tender sexual relationship of Perdita and Florizel.

Other themes that we have explored in Shakespeare find their most precise expression in this scene. Leontes addresses the 'statue':

> ...O royal piece,
> There's magic in thy majesty, which has...
> From thy admiring daughters took the spirits...[28]

---

[27] Sonnet 123.   [28] v. iii. 38 et seq.

The first of Shakespeare's answers to the problems of time was the miracle of reproduction, as we saw in the Sonnets. But there Shakespeare had seen only the biological rebirth: the replication of one's flesh comforted but did not present a spiritual answer. An old man could 'see' his 'blood warm' when he feels it 'cold'.[29] But here the spirit of Perdita, the younger generation, seems to have been breathed into the statue of Hermione: the rebirth is a spiritual one. The ageing process of time seems to have been made irrelevant, though it must still operate.

The 'statue' is also, perhaps, a symbol of Shakespeare's art. We saw how in *Twelfth Night* the dead masks of Olivia, Orsino, and Viola are stripped away to reveal the person beneath. When the 'statue' comes alive the effect is similar to the unmaskings that are characteristic of the great comedies. A lifeless and deceptive outward seeming is replaced by the living reality, rather as a stage 'type' gives way to a genuine dramatic personality. The great sculptor, Julio Romano,[30] is in some respects the dramatist himself, who is able to work the miracle of Pygmalion and bring his sculptures to life. The awakening of the 'statue' is like the unmaskings of Rosalind and Viola, which similarly open the eyes of the main characters in their plays. Viola's pose of manhood and Hermione's imitation of stone are both powerful ritual masks, which profoundly alter and adjust the perception of those who witness their unmasking.

Another theme which we examined in *Twelfth Night* was the idea of temporal appropriateness: that a true relationship with time consisted in being at harmony with the present moment. This implied that one must sometimes wait for the opportunity to achieve one's desires, that time had a certain texture which denied one's wishes at one moment, but permitted them at another; as Brutus puts it:

> There is a tide in the affairs of men
> Which, taken at the flood, leads on to fortune;
> Omitted, all the voyage of their life
> Is bound in shallows and in miseries.[31]

[29] Sonnet 2.
[30] I feel sure that the pornographic excursions of the historical Julio Romano have no relevance here!   [31] *Julius Caesar*, IV. iii. 216 et seq.

One must be prepared, when the opportunity comes, to take it with both hands. Viola must wait several months 'like Patience on a monument'[32] until her opportunity arises: but when it does come, both she and her brother are unequivocally committed to it. Leontes must wait sixteen years: but when he sees the 'statue' he realizes that the opportunity he has been waiting for, of regaining his wife, is now or never. Paulina tests him by offering to cover the 'statue' and lead him away: but he hangs on to his happiness once he has found it. Hamlet, too, possessed this sense of temporal appropriateness when he prepared himself for the duel with Laertes. Macbeth wanted his predicted crown at once, and could not wait till time brought it to him; and his crime broke the laws not only of human society, but also of time itself. ' 'Tis time', says Paulina, 'descend; be stone no more . . .'; time can bring an opportunity of expiation, even of a crime like Leontes'.

By the end of Shakespeare's dramatic career he seems to have come to terms with time. The destroyer, devourer, and tyrant of the Sonnets has become a more mysterious but less malignant force. 'Be cheerful, sir', says Prospero to Ferdinand:

> Our revels now are ended. These our actors,
> As I foretold you, were all spirits, and
> Are melted into air, into thin air;
> And, like the baseless fabric of this vision,
> The cloud-capp'd towers, the gorgeous palaces,
> The solemn temples, the great globe itself,
> Yea, all which it inherit, shall dissolve,
> And, like this insubstantial pageant faded,
> Leave not a rack behind. We are such stuff
> As dreams are made on; and our little life
> Is rounded with a sleep. Sir, I am vex'd;
> Bear with my weakness; my old brain is troubled;
> Be not disturb'd with my infirmity.
> If you be pleas'd, retire into my cell
> And there repose; a turn or two I'll walk
> To still my beating mind.
> *Mir:* } We wish your peace.[33]
> *Fer:* }

---

[32] *Twelfth Night*, II. iv. 113.   [33] *The Tempest*, IV. i. 148 et seq.

Time is no longer a problem for a poet who could write such lines of acceptance of transience, and who made the statue of the dead beloved breathe and move.

Appendix

The Greek Philosophers

Of the pre-Socratic philosophers the mysterious and elliptical fragments of Herakleitos (fifth century B.C.) that are preserved make
interesting reading on this subject. For Herakleitos, being itself is
flux, energy, or movement:

Everything flows and nothing abides; everything gives way and noth-
ing stays fixed (Fragment 20).
You cannot step twice into the same river, for other waters are continually flowing on (Fragment 21).
Cool things become warm, the warm grows cool; the moist dries, the
parched becomes moist (Fragment 22).
It is in changing that things find repose (Fragment 23).
Time is a child moving counters in a game; the royal power is a
child's (Fragment 24).
War is both father and king of all . . . (Fragment 25).
It should be understood that war is the common condition, that strife
is justice, and that all things come to pass through the compulsion of
strife (Fragment 26).
Homer was wrong in saying, 'Would that strife might perish from
among gods and men.' For if that were to occur, then all things would
cease to exist (Fragment 27).
This universe, which is the same for all, has not been made by any
god or man, but it has always been, is, and will be—an ever-living fire,
kindling itself by regular measures and going out by regular measures
(Fragment 29).
There is an exchange of all things for fire and of fire for all things, as
there is of wares for gold and of gold for wares (Fragment 28).
Fire lives in the death of earth, air in the death of fire, water in the
death of air, and earth in the death of water (Fragment 34).
Fire in its advance will judge and overtake all things (Fragment 72).
Opposition brings concord. Out of discord comes the fairest harmony
(Fragment 98).
The way up and the way down are one and the same (Fragment
108).
In the circle the beginning and the end are common (Fragment 109;

Einstein's curved space seems to mirror the drift of these last two statements).

People do not understand how that which is at variance with itself agrees with itself. There is a harmony in the bending back, as in the case of the bow and the lyre. (Fragment 114).

The name of the bow is life, but its work is death (Fragment 115).

The hidden harmony is better than the obvious (Fragment 116).

All things come in their due seasons (Fragment 123).

These fragments have been taken from Philip Wheelwright's translation in his *Heraclitus* (Princeton University Press, 1959). The numbering is also his.

Much of what Plato (427–347 B.C.) has to say about time may be found in the *Timaeus*. For Plato the factors required to explain the cosmos adequately are three: the world of change, flux, and becoming; the container and materials of change, ordered by the Demiurge; and the ideal and incorruptible pattern of eternity. What is important for our purposes is the distinction he makes between time and eternity, and the fact that he locates Being in the things that are changed, rather than in the process of change: 'The work of the creator, whenever he looks to the unchangeable and fashions the form and nature of his work after an unchangeable pattern, must necessarily be made fair and perfect; but when he looks to the created only and uses a created pattern, it is not fair or perfect' (p. 28 in Stephanus's edition of Plato [Paris, 1578]). These quotations are taken from the third edition of Benjamin Jowett's translation, reprinted in New York by the Liberal Arts Press, 1949. This edition keeps the pagination of Stephanus.

When the Father and Creator saw the creature which he had made moving and living, the created image of the eternal gods, he rejoiced, and in his joy determined to make the copy still more like the original; and as this was eternal, he sought to make the universe eternal, so far as might be. Now the nature of the ideal being was everlasting, but to bestow this attribute in its fullness upon a creature was impossible. Wherefore he resolved to have a moving image of eternity, and when he set in order the heaven, he made this image eternal but moving according to number, while eternity itself rests in unity; and this image we call time. For there were no days and nights and months and years before the heaven was created, but when he constructed the heaven he constructed them also. They are all parts of time, and the past and future are created species of time, which we unconsciously but wrongly transfer to the eternal essence; for we say that he 'was', he 'is', he 'will be', but the truth is that 'is' alone is properly attributed to him, and that 'was' and 'will be' are only to be spoken of becoming in time, for they are motions. But that which is immovably the same cannot become older or younger by time, nor ever did or has become, or hereafter will be, older or younger, nor is subject at all to any of those states which affect moving and sensible things and of which generation is the cause. These are the forms of time, which imitates eternity and revolves according to the law of number. Moreover, when we say that what has become *is* become and what becomes *is* becoming, and that what will become *is* about to become and that the non-existent *is* non-existent—all these are inaccurate modes of expression (pp. 37–8).

Aristotle (384–322 B.C.) devotes a large subsection of the Physics to the nature of time, and much more to the idea of motion, which he closely connects with time. However, he seems to have become trapped in an insoluble and irreconcilable contradiction, inherent in the ambiguity of the word 'time'. For time can either be motion, flux, and change, or the milieu within which they take place. Aristotle wrestles with this problem, attempting to find a definition of time that will cover both these senses. First, 'clearly' time 'is not movement' (*Physics*, book IV, 10, 218^{b}19). Next, time is not 'independent of movement' (219^{a}1). Then time is 'something that belongs to movement' (219^{a}8). But now 'time is directly the measure of motion' (223^{a}15), and 'time is measured by motion as well as motion by time' (223^{b}15).

The only way out of the problem is simply to recognize two different senses of time. What comes out of Aristotle's difficulty, however, is an emphasis on the present moment, which will be taken up by some of his successors. For these quotations I have used the translation by R. P. Hardie and R. K. Gaye in the W. D. Ross edition of the *Works*, 1930 (reprinted 1966).

Though it is highly unlikely that Shakespeare had read any of the Greek philosophers, nevertheless what they said about time was inevitably part of the intellectual syntax of his period. Furthermore, their ideas might have come to him indirectly through a multitude of channels, for instance Pierre de la Primaudaye's *French Academic*, translated in 1594 by 'T.B.', or Marcellus Palingenius Stellatus' *Zodiake of Life*, translated by Barnaby Googe in 1588. Again, many of the classical concepts of time were expressed in emblems and allegorical works of art. Erwin Panofsky's *Studies in Iconology*, 1939, contains a fascinating discussion of Father Time, who could be at once the devourer, the creator, the revealer, the moment of opportunity, and the judge of action. Herakleitos' vision of time, in which life and death are reconciled by harmony or tension, is echoed by allegorical paintings in the Renaissance where Father Time contains elements both from 'aion', the ancient Iranian principle of creativity, and also from Cronus, the Greek god who devoured his children. Plato's distinction between time and eternity was likewise a commonplace of popular and religious art.

The Philosophy of Rome

Sidney Lee, in *Elizabethan and Other Essays*, selected and edited by F. S. Boas (1928), pp. 116–40, and J. B. Leishman, throughout his *Themes and Variations in Shakespeare's Sonnets* (1961), have discussed in detail the debt Shakespeare owes to classical literature and its continental descendants, with respect to the moods and images he uses to express his ideas of time. But literature intersects philosophy: what developments in the basic ideas of time took place under the aegis of Rome?

Unlike the Greek philosophy, much of Roman thought may have been directly available to Shakespeare in the form of translations. The 'Golden Boke' of Marcus Aurelius Antonius (A.D. 121–80) as the *Meditations* were called, was translated by John Bourchier in 1534; it went through ten editions by 1586. In the *Meditations* the philosophy of time has become more directly ethical in its nature: time is no longer only an object of investigation, but is now also a force in human life to which we must make moral adjustments:

This is the whole matter: see always how ephemeral and cheap are the things of man—yesterday, a spot of albumen, to-morrow, ashes or a mummy. Therefore make your passage through this span of time in obedience to Nature and gladly lay down your life, as an olive, when ripe, might fall, blessing her who bare it and grateful to the tree which gave it life (A. S. L. Farquharson, trans. and ed., *The Meditations of Marcus Aurelius Antoninus*, 1944, vol. 1, p. 71).

Be like the headland on which the waves continually break, but it stands firm and about it the boiling waters sink to sleep . . . 'lucky am I, because, though this befell me, I continue free from sorrow, neither crushed by the present, nor fearing what is to come' (pp. 71–3).

In the conviction that it is possible you may depart from life at once, act and speak and think in every case accordingly. (p. 27).

. . . each of us lives only in the present, this brief moment; the rest is either a life that is past, or is in an uncertain future (p. 45).

Perfection of character possesses this: to live each day as if the last, to be neither feverish nor apathetic, and not to act a part (p. 145).

It is in your power to secure at once all the objects which you dream of reaching by a roundabout path, if you will be fair to yourself: that is, if you will leave all the past behind, commit the future to Providence and direct the present, and that alone, to Holiness and Justice (p. 235).

Plotinus (A.D. 205?–270) follows Plato in his emphasis on time as transcended by eternity; but he introduces a new notion of time, as essentially a subjective phenomenon. Time for him is 'the Life of the Soul in movement as it passes from one stage of act or experience to another' (the *Third Ennead,* tractate 7, c. 11): 'Time . . . is not to be conceived as outside of soul' (III. 7. 11). This idea is revolutionary: it is not essentially different from Kant's view of time as one of the categories of perception. For these quotations I have used the third edition of Stephen MacKenna's translation (1962; first published by the Medici Society, 1917–30).

St. Augustine of Hippo (A.D. 345–430) is largely responsible for the traditional Christian attitude towards time that we still find in the pulpit, in popular works of theology, and even in Christian poetry such as T. S. Eliot's *Four Quartets.* His radical separation of the world of man from the world of God is based on a sharp division between time and eternity. In many ways the early Christian sense of the spiritual had been one of immanence, of the presence of their God invisibly among them in the world. Augustine's God is remote, incomprehensible, transcendent: '. . . the word is spoken from all eternity, and in it are all things spoken eternally. For that which is spoken doth not grow to an end, nor is the one thing said that the next may be spoken, but all things at once and eternally. For otherwise there would be time and so mutation, and no true eternity nor true immortality' (Sir Tobie Matthew, Kt., trans., *The Confessions of St. Augustine,* revised and emended Dom Roger Hudleston, 1954, bk. 11, p. 334).

What did God do before he made heaven and earth? . . . They that talk in such a fashion as this, do not yet understand Thee, . . . nor yet do they understand how those things are made, which are made by Thee and in Thee; and they strive to have some relish of things eternal while their heart—as yet unstable withal—doth flicker to and fro in the motions of things past and to come. Who shall be able to hold and fix it, that for a while it may be still, and may catch a glimpse of thy ever-fixed eternity, and compare it with the times that never stand, that so he may see how these things are not to be compared together? That he may understand how a long time is not made long, but out of many transitory motions, which cannot be extended all at once; but that all the while there passeth nothing in eternity, where all is present; but that no time can be present all at once. And that he may see that all time which is past is driven away by that time which is to come; and that all time which is to come follows upon that which is past; and that all which is both past and future is created, and doth flow out from that which is always present. Who shall hold fast the heart of a man that it may stand and see how that eternity which ever standeth still, doth dictate the times both past and future, whilst yet itself is neither past nor future? (bk. 11, pp. 337–8).

What is of particular interest here is Augustine's identification of eternity with the present: in eternity there is no duration; an eternal being is present to himself in all his stages and aspects. The corollary of this is that if we wish to apprehend the spiritual and the eternal, we must do it through the infinitesimal and fleeting moment of the present: ' . . . as for the present, if it could be for ever present and not pass on to become time past, truly it should not be time but eternity' (bk. 11, p. 341). Again, for Augustine, as with Plato and Marcus Aurelius, time past and time future have no real existence.

It is this model of the philosophical universe, divided into the 'secular' or 'temporal' on one hand, and the eternal and spiritual on the other, which formed the centre of medieval theology. After Augustine it remained only for Boethius (A.D. 480?–524?) to discuss and define the forces which mediate between the two worlds—Fate and Providence; and to refine the Stoic ethic of co-operation with one's appointed destiny into Christian collaboration with Providence. There is an element of this sense of acceptance in Hamlet's final answer to the problems that confront him, as I have pointed out.

The English Literary Tradition

Shakespeare lived in a country which had always been peculiarly conscious of the fall of great civilizations, the ruins of a noble past, the onrush of the seasons towards winter, and the miracle of spring. Time for the English seems always to have been associated with a feeling neither of despair nor optimism, but rather of gentle and melancholy elegy. Their emotional sense of natural time is a mixture of the Mediterranean sense of recurrence and the Norse sense of catastrophe; of continuity and Ragnarok. We find this mixture of recurrence and catastrophe in the Old English poem, *The Seafarer*:

> Blossoms take the woods, the towns grow fair,
> the fields are in flower, fast goes the world:
> all those move the man whose mood is bent,

whose thought is ready, who thinks even so
to fare afar, on the flood to ride.
And the cuckoo warns with woeful voice,
summer's ward sings, sorrow he heralds,
bitter, in breast-hoard . . .

So, now, my soul soars from my bosom,
the mood of my mind moves with the sea-flood,
over the home of the whale, high flies and wide
to the ends of the earth . . .

Dearer, then, to me
the boons of the Lord than this life that is dead
in a land that passes; I believe no whit
that earthly weal is everlasting.

The passing of the seasons, the fall of ancient empires, and the ageing
and death of the individual are closely associated:

Gone is all this glory, all; glee is departed.
The weaker walk this world and hold it,
spend it in hardship; splendour is stricken,
earthly honour ages and withers,
so now each of men through middle-earth:
eld fares on him, his face turns pale,
the greybeard grieves; his good friends of yore,
begotten of athelings, he knows given to earth.
(Kemp Malone's translation, ll. 48–93.)

In Wulfstan's *Sermo Lupi ad Anglos* the preacher warns his flock
specifically by means of the examples of the civilizations of Rome
and of the Britons, which passed away leaving only their huge
inexplicable ruins.

The unknown poet of *Sir Gawaine and the Green Knight* evokes
a similar mood in the passage where the year passes swiftly that is to
bring the courteous knight to his doom:

For thaʒ men ben mery in mynde quen they han mayn drynk,
A ʒere ʒernes ful ʒerne, and ʒeldeʒ neuer lyke,
The forme to the fynisment foldeʒ ful selden.
Forthi this Zol overʒede, and the ʒere after,
And uche sesoun serlepes sued after other . . .
. . . Wela wynne is the wort that waxes theroute,
When the donkande dewe dropeʒ of the leueʒ,

To bide a blysful blusch of the bry3t sunne.
Bot then hy3es heruest, and hardene3 hym sore,
Warne3 hym for the wynter to wax ful rype . . .
. . . Wrothe wynde of the welkyn wrastele3 with the sunne,
The leue3 lancen fro the lynde and ly3ten on the grounde,
And al grayes the gres that gren wat3 ere;
Thenne all rype3 and rote3 that ros upon fyrst,
And thus 3irnes the 3ere in 3isterdayes mony,
And wynter wynde3 agayn . . .

(J. R. R. Tolkien and E. V. Gordon eds., *Sir Gawaine and The Green Knight*, 1955, ll. 497 et seq. I have used 'th' for 'thorn' throughout.)

These last few lines sound very Shakespearean: 'Then all ripes and rots that rose at first, and thus the year passes with its many yesterdays, and winter returns . . .' We can compare this with several passages in the sonnets.

Medieval English drama contains many of these elements: in the Moralities, for instance, the inevitability of death and the transience of worldly goods and worldly glory. The cycle plays, with their assumption that a divine plan is working in history, show a different aspect of time: as governed by providence, and as containing a Christian teleology.

At the end of Thomas Malory's *Morte D'Arthur* there is the same elegiac mood, and the same feeling of the passing of a golden age, that we have seen in the Anglo-Saxons:

And when Sir Ector heard such noise and light in the choir of Joyous Gard, he alit and put his horse from him, and came into the choir; and there he saw men sing and weep. And all they knew Sir Ector, but he knew not them. Then went Sir Bors unto Sir Ector, and told him how there lay his brother, Sir Lancelot, dead; and then Sir Ector threw his shield, sword, and helm from him. And when he beheld Sir Lancelot's visage, he fell down in a swoon. And when he waked it were hard any tongue to tell the doleful complaints that he made for his brother. 'Ah, Lancelot,' he said, 'thou were head of all Christian knights, and now I dare say,' said Sir Ector, 'thou, Sir Lancelot, there thou liest, that thou were never matched of earthly knight's hand. And thou were the courteousest knight that ever bore shield. And thou were the truest friend to thy lover that ever bestrode horse. And thou were the truest lover, of a sinful man, that ever loved woman. And thou were the kindest man that ever struck with sword. And thou were the goodliest person that ever came among press of knights. And thou was the meekest man and the gentlest that ever ate in hall among ladies. And thou were the sternest knight to thy mortal foe that ever put spear in the breast.' Then there was weeping and dolour out of measure' (book xxi, chapter 13).

The Arthurian synthesis of religious and secular virtues, and of social and personal forces, is broken by death in this passage. It cannot survive in this world, because the world of time is at war with eternity, and what has been created by time must end in time.

Shakespeare's Contemporaries

In Shakespeare's time many of the elements I have sketched above came together. In Louis Leroy's *Of the Interchangeable Course or Variety of Things in the Whole World*, translated by Robert Ashley in 1594, we find a blending of the Platonic sense of sublunary imperfection and mutability with the Christian teleology; he felt that one of the great cycles of history, the 'great year' (a term borrowed from Plato) was due to come to an end in 1604; here he describes his idea: 'There are certaine periods appointed for the world; which while they endure, all thinges do come to their vigour; and which being ended, they do al perish: but . . . al of them end their course within the revolution of the great year' (Loys le Roy [called Ludovicus Regius], *Of the Interchangeable Course or Variety of Things in the Whole World*, trans. Robert Ashley, 1594, f. B.2. verso). This sense of doom occurs also in John Norden's complicated and astrological *Vicissitudo Rerum*:

> The *Priests* of *Egypt* gazing on the starres,
> Are sayd to see the *Worlds* sad ruines past,
> That had beted by *fire* and *Waters* iarres:
> And how the *World* inconstant and unchaste,
> Assayed by these, cannot alike stand fast . . .
> (*Shakespeare Association Facsimiles,* no. 4., 1931, stanza 37.)

But what is of particular interest is the way that the objective, impersonal forces of time become humanized and subjectivized in the Renaissance. The huge movements of cosmic doomsday become an image of the changes of the human heart:

> When all this All doth pass from age to age,
> And revolution in a circle turn,
> Then heavenly Justice doth appear like rage,
> The caves do roar, the very seas do burn,
> Glory grows dark, the sun become a night,
> And makes this great world feel a greater might.

When Love doth change his seat from heart to heart,
And worth about the wheel of fortune goes,
Grace is diseased, desert seems overthwart,
Vows are forlorn, and truth doth credit lose,
Chance then gives law, desire must be wise
And look more ways than one, or lose her eyes ...

The parallelism of these two stanzas from Fulke Greville's *Caelica*, no. 69 ('When all this All'), is a clear indication of the direction of the Renaissance mind with respect to time. Time exists both in the natural world and in the human soul; and as in nature it destroys and corrupts the things of earth, so in man it operates as a force of moral decay. The only way to avoid this corruption is with Greville as with Shakespeare, to become independent of Time:

The world, that all contains, is ever moving;
The stars within their spheres forever turned;
Nature, the queen of change, to change is loving;
And form to matter new is still adjourned.

Fortune, our fancy-God, to vary liketh;
Place is not bound to things within it placed;
The present time upon time passëd striketh;
With Phoebus' wandering course the earth is graced.

The air still moves, and by its moving cleareth;
The fire up ascends, and planets feedeth;
The water passeth on, and all lets weareth;
The earth stands still, yet change of changes breedeth.

Her plants, which summer ripes, in winter fade;
Each creature in inconstant mother lieth;
Man made of earth, and for whom earth is made,
Still dying lives, and living ever dieth.
Only like fate sweet Myra never varies,
Yet in her eyes the doom of all change carries.   (*Caelica*, no. 7.)

This extraordinarily beautiful poem, with its swift, relentless feminine rhymes, its continuous movement, and its powerful evocation of transience, contains many of the themes we have found in the thought of Greece and Rome. We must conclude either that Greville was an immensely learned man, or that second-hand versions of these ideas must have been readily available. In his *Treatie of Warres* the philosophies of Herakleitos and Plato come together with the transcendental theology of Augustine and the native English sense of time; and again, there is the continual reference to the human viewpoint:

All which best root, and spring in new foundations
Of States, or Kingdoms; and againe in age,
Or height of pride, and power feele declination;
Mortality is Changes proper stage:
States have degrees, and humane bodies have,
Springs, Summer, Autumn, winter, and the grave ...
(Geoffrey Bullough, ed., *The Poems and Dramas of Fulke Greville,*
1939, vol I, p. 224.)

Now as the *Warres* prove mans mortality;
So doe the oppositions here below,
Of Elements, the contrariety
Of Constellations, which above doe shew,
Of qualities in flesh, will in the spirit;
Principles of discord, not of concord made,
All prove God meant not Man should here inherit
A *time-made* world, which with time should not fade;
But as *Noes flood* once drown'd woods, hils, & plain,
So should the fire of *Christ* waste all againe.
(Ibid., p. 225; Bullough thinks the poem was written between 1597 and
1610. See op. cit., pp. 67–72.)

There is the same identification of cosmic with human change in
Montaigne's essay *Of Repenting,* which was translated with the other
Essaies in 1603 by John Florio:

The world runnes all on wheeles. All things therein moove without
intermission; yea the earth, the rockes of Caucasus, and the Pyramides of
Ægypt, both with the publike and their own motion. *Constancy it self is
nothing but a languishing and wavering dance.* I cannot settle my object;
it goeth so unquietly and staggering, with a natural drunkennesse ... I
describe not the essence, but the passage; not a passage from age to age,
or as the people reckon, from seaven yeares to seaven; but from day to
day, from minute to minute. My history must be fitted to the present. I
may soone change, not onely fortune, but intention. It is a counterrule
[in French, 'contrerolle': 'assortment', 'jumble'] of divers and variable
accidents, and irresolute imaginations, and sometimes contrary: whether
it be that my selfe am other, or that I apprehend subjects, by other
circumstances and considerations (John Florio, trans., *The Essays of
Montaigne,* ed. J. I. M. Stewart, 1931, vol. II, p. 194).

'I describe not the essence, but the passage.' This is a manifesto of
human time as opposed to the theorizing of the philosophers; and
it comes nearest of all, perhaps, to Shakespeare's own artistic viewpoint in the poems and plays.

List of Works Consulted

Editions of the Text

I have used Peter Alexander's edition of the *Complete Works*, Tudor Edition, 1964 (1951), for all quotations and references, as it is a good standard edition and the line numbers correspond to those of the great Cambridge edition of Clark and Wright.

For closer textual work the *New Variorum* has been used, and the *New Arden* edition has been consulted for its notes.

C. T. Onions' *Shakespeare Glossary* has also been useful.

General

ANTONINUS, MARCUS AURELIUS, *The Meditations*, ed. and trans. A. S. L. Farquharson, 2 vols. Oxford: The Clarendon Press, 1944.

ARISTOTLE, *Physics*, trans. R. P. Hardie and R. K. Gaye, in vol. II of the *Works*, under the editorship of J. A. Smith and W. D. Ross. Oxford: The Clarendon Press, 1930.

ST. AUGUSTINE OF HIPPO, *The Confessions*, trans. Sir Tobie Matthew, Kt., revised and emended by Dom Roger Hudleston. London: Orchard Books: Burns & Oates, 1954.

BARBER, C. L., *Shakespeare's Festive Comedy*. Princeton University Press, 1959.

BERGSON, HENRY, *Time and Free Will*, trans. F. L. Pogson. London: S. Sonnenschein & Co., Ltd., 1910.

BETHELL, S. L., *The Winter's Tale, a Study*. London: Staples Press, 1947.

BOSWELL-STONE, W. G., *Shakespeare's Holinshed*. London: Lawrence & Bullen, 1896.

BRADLEY, A. C., *Shakespearean Tragedy*. London: Macmillan & Co., Ltd., 1914 (1904).

CECIL, LORD DAVID, *The Fine Art of Reading*. Indianapolis, New York: Bobbs-Merrill Co., 1957.

CLEMEN, WOLFGANG H., *The Development of Shakespeare's Imagery*. London: Methuen & Co., 1951.

COLERIDGE, S. T., *Seven Lectures on Shakespeare and Milton*: transcript of notes by J. P. Collier at Coleridge's lectures, 1811–12. London: Chapman & Hall, 1856.

COLLINGWOOD, R. G., *The Idea of Nature*. Oxford: The Clarendon Press, 1945.

'B. E. GENT.', *A New Dictionary of the Terms Ancient and Modern of the Canting Crew*. London: W. Hawes, 1699.

ELIOT, T. S., *Four Quartets*. London: Faber & Faber, 1964 (1944).

—— *Collected Plays*. London: Faber & Faber, 1962.

——*Collected Poems*, 1909–1962. London: Faber & Faber, 1963.

EWBANK, I. S., 'The Triumph of Time in *The Winter's Tale'*, *Review of English Literature*, no. 5, 1964.

FLORIO, JOHN, trans., *The Essays of Montaigne*, ed. J. I. M. Stewart, 2 vols. London: The Nonesuch Press, 1931.

GARRETT, W. P., ed., *More Talking about Shapespeare*. London: Longmans, Green, & Co., 1959.

GRENVILLE, FULKE, LORD BROOKE, *The Poems and Dramas*, ed. Geoffrey Bullough. Edinburgh: Oliver & Boyd, 1939.

HOLTZ, WILLIAM, 'Time's Chariot and *Tristram Shandy'*, in *Michigan Quarterly Review*, vol. v., Summer 1966.

JOHNSON, SAMUEL, *Dictionary of the English Language*. London: C. & J. Rivington, 1824 (1755).

KENNER, HUGH, *The Counterfeiters*. Bloomington, Indiana, and London: Indiana University Press, 1968.

KITTREDGE, G. L., *Witchcraft in Old and New England*. Cambridge, Massachusetts: Harvard University Press, 1929.

KNIGHT, G. WILSON, *The Crown of Life*. London: Methuen & Co., 1948 (1947).

—— *The Shakespearean Tempest*. London: Methuen & Co., 1953 (1932).

—— *The Imperial Theme*. London: Methuen & Co., 1954 (1931).

KNIGHTS, L. C., *An Approach to Hamlet*. London: Chatto & Windus, 1960.

LAING, R. D., *The Divided Self*. London: Tavistock Publications, 1960.

—— *The Politics of Experience*. London: Penguin Books, 1967.

LEACH, E. R., *Rethinking Anthropology*. London: Athlone Press, 1961.

LEAVIS, F. R., *The Common Pursuit*. London: Chatto & Windus, 1952.

LEE, SIR SIDNEY, *Elizabethan and Other Essays*, selected and ed. by F. S. Boas. Oxford: The Clarendon Press, 1929.

LEISHMAN, J. B., *Themes and Variations in Shakespeare's Sonnets*. London: Hutchinson, 1961.

LEROY, LOYS (LUDOVICUS REGIUS), *Of the Interchangeable Course, or Variety of Things in the Whole World*, trans. Robert Ashley. London: C. Yetsweirt, 1594.

MANN, THOMAS, *The Magic Mountain*, trans. H. T. Lowe-Porter. New York: Alfred A. Knopf, 1939.

MUIR, KENNETH, *William Shakespeare: the Great Tragedies*, London: Longmans, Green & Co., 1961. (Bibliographical Series of Supplements to *British Book News*, no. 133.)

MURRY, J. MIDDLETON, *Shakespeare*. London: Jonathan Cape, 1965 (1936).

NORDEN, JOHN, *Vicissitudo Rerum*, 1600. *Shakespeare Association Facsimile*, no. 4. London: Oxford University Press, 1931.

PARTRIDGE, ERIC, *Shakespeare's Bawdy*. London: Routledge & Kegan Paul, 1955.

PLATO, *Timaeus*, trans. B. Jowett. New York: Liberal Arts Press, 1949. (Also in *The Dialogues of Plato*, trans. B. Jowett, 5 vols. Oxford: The Clarendon Press, 1892 (1868–71).)

PLOTINUS, *Enneads*, trans. S. MacKenna. London: Faber & Faber, 1962 (1917–30).

POULET, GEORGES, *Études sur le temps humain*. Edinburgh University Press, 1949.

ROSSITER, A. P., *Angel with Horns*, ed. Graham Storey. London: Longmans, Green, & Co., 1961.

SEWELL, WILLIAM ARTHUR, *Character and Society in Shakespeare*. Oxford: The Clarendon Press, 1951.

SPENSER, EDMUND, *Complete Works*, ed. T. C. Smith and E. De Selincourt. London: Oxford University Press, 1952 (1909).

SPURGEON, CAROLINE F. E., *Shakespeare's Imagery and What It Tells Us*. Cambridge: University Press, 1935.

STEWART, J. I. M., *Character and Motive in Shakespeare*. London: Longmans, Green & Co., 1949.

STOLL, E. E., 'Source and Motive in *Macbeth* and *Othello*' in *Review of English Studies*, xix (1943), 25.

TILLYARD, E. M. W., *Shakespeare's Last Plays*. London: Chatto & Windus, 1951 (1938).

TOLKIEN, J. R. R., and GORDON, E. V., eds., *Sir Gawaine and the Green Knight*. Oxford: The Clarendon Press, 1955 (1925).

TURNER, V. W., *The Forest of Symbols: Aspects of Ndembu Ritual*. Cornell University Press, 1967.

——*The Drums of Affliction*. Oxford: The Clarendon Press, 1968.

—— *The Ritual Process: Structure and Anti-Structure*. Chicago University Press, 1969.

Index

PRINTED IN GREAT BRITAIN
AT THE UNIVERSITY PRESS, OXFORD
BY VIVIAN RIDLER
PRINTER TO THE UNIVERSITY